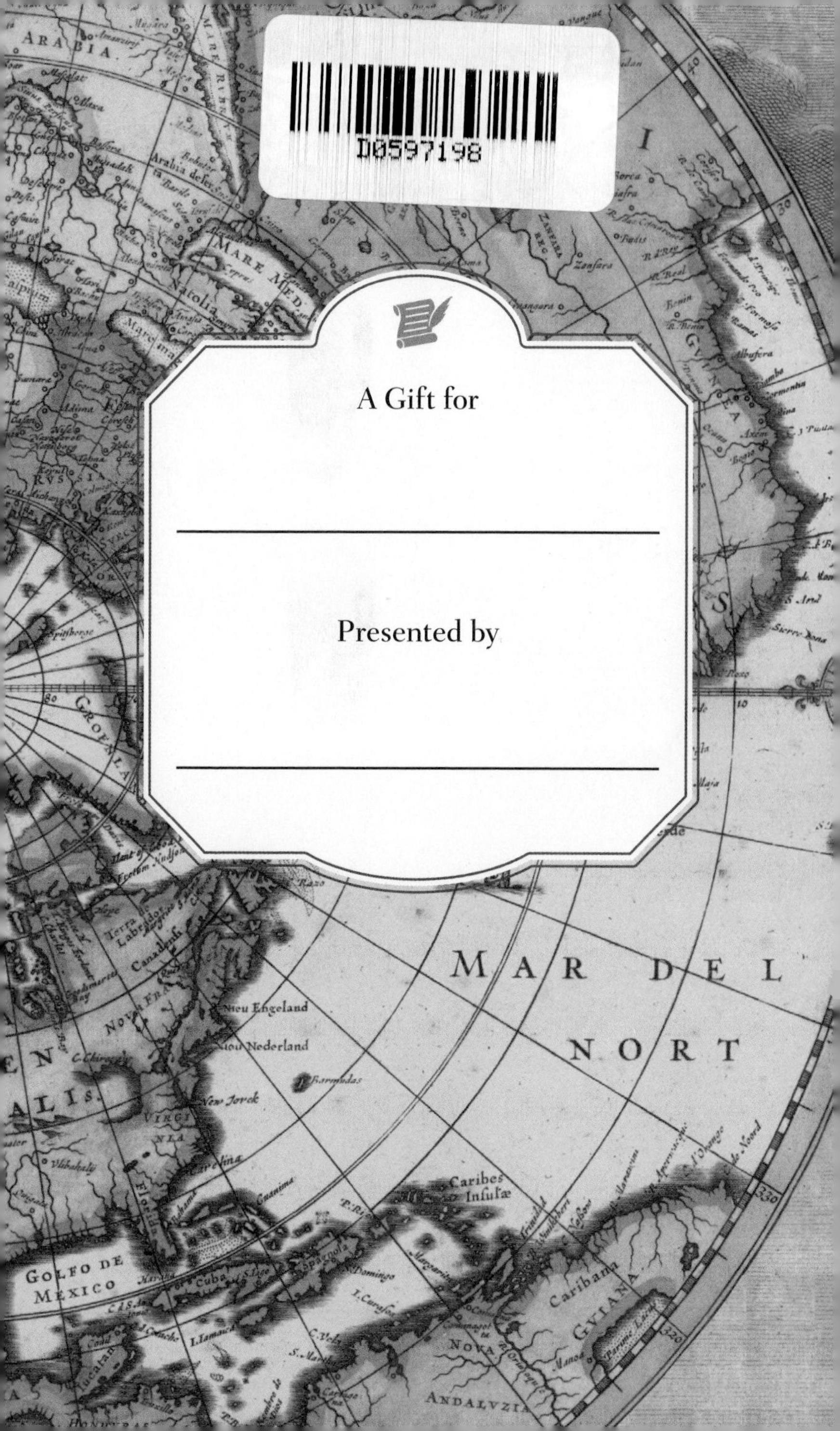
D0597198
A Gift for
Presented by
MAR DEL
NORT
GOLFO DE
MEXICO
Nieu Engeland
Nieu Nederland
New Jorck
Caribes
Insulæ
Cuba
Caribana
GVIANA
NOVA
ANDALVZIA
Natolia
ARABIA

I Used to Know That

WORLD HISTORY

The supreme purpose of history
is a better world.

—Herbert Hoover (1874–1964)

I Used to Know That
WORLD HISTORY

Intriguing Facts About
the World's Greatest Empires,
Leaders, Cultures, and Conflicts

Emma Marriott

The Reader's Digest Association, Inc.
New York, NY / Montreal

For Robin, and his uncanny ability to remember stuff.

A READER'S DIGEST BOOK

First published in Great Britain by Michael O'Mara Books Limited, 9 Lion Yard, Tremadoc Road, London SW47NQ.

FOR READER'S DIGEST
U.S. Editor: Barbara Booth
Consulting Editor: Andrea Chesman
Designer: Nick Anderson
Illustrator: Andrew Pinder
Manager, English Book Editorial, Reader's Digest Canada: Pamela Johnson
Senior Art Director: George McKeon
Associate Publisher, Trade Publishing: Rosanne McManus
President and Publisher, Trade Publishing: Harold Clarke
Editor-in-Chief, Reader's Digest North America: Liz Vaccariello
President, Reader's Digest North America: Dan Lagani
President and CEO, Reader's Digest Association, Inc.: Robert H. Guth

Library of Congress Cataloging in Publication Data
Marriott, Emma.
I used to know that. World history : Intriguing Facts about the World's Greatest Empires, Leaders, Cultures, and Conflicts / Emma Marriott.
p. cm.
"A Reader's Digest book"–T.p. verso.
Includes bibliographical references and index.
ISBN 978-1-60652-459-6 – ISBN 978-1-60652-460-2 (epub) – ISBN 978-1-60652-461-9 (adobe)
1. World history. 2. Europe–History. I. Title. II. Title: World history.
D23.M357 2012
909-dc23
2011037072

We are committed to both the quality of our products and the service we provide to our customers. We value your comments, so please feel free to contact us.

The Reader's Digest Association, Inc.
Adult Trade Publishing
44 S. Broadway
White Plains, NY 10601

For more Reader's Digest products and information, visit our website:
www.rd.com (in the United States)
www.readersdigest.ca (in Canada)

Printed in the United States

1 3 5 7 9 10 8 6 4 2

Contents

Introduction

History is arguably one of the most important subjects taught at school. Every current affairs story you read in the paper or watch on the news is somehow linked to the past. History, far from being a dusty subject, is potent and sometimes dangerous (see Nazi Germany). In the words of George Santayana, "Those who cannot remember the past are condemned to repeat it."

This book aims to fill in all the crucial and rather embarrassing gaps in your knowledge of world history, however they got there. Key areas, stretching right back to the beginnings of civilization, are covered succinctly but comprehensively. This is emphatically not an academic tome: You might find the odd enlivening quotation, but you won't find great reams of primary sources (life, and this book, is simply too short). Instead, here are the essentials of the history you really should know, as well as a few extra nuggets that might surprise you (did you know, for example, that Mussolini used to be an elementary school teacher?).

I hope *I Used to Know That: World History* helps flesh out your hazier classroom memories and reignites a passion for the past—and that you get as much enjoyment out of reading it as I had researching and writing it.

Stick to your own wall, I'm concentrating.

Chapter 1

Early Civilizations

Early man was a nomadic hunter-gatherer. But sometime between 8000 B.C. and 3000 B.C., people began to raise plants and domesticate animals. As agricultural societies began to generate food surpluses, some people were freed to build, invent, create tools, and make clothing. Civilization began to emerge.

The first signs of civilization developed in the fertile land of Mesopotamia between the Tigris and the Euphrates rivers at around 5000 B.C. Other civilizations grew along the banks of the Nile, culminating in ancient Egypt, and along the Indus River in India and in the Yellow River valley in China.

Why along rivers? Periodic flooding along the shores renewed the farmland and allowed farmers to grow surpluses. The rivers also provided water for human consumption and trade. Beyond the fertile river valleys, the land was mostly mountainous or desert—not at all conducive to farming.

Pre-Classical Civilizations

The early civilizations that rose and fell were characterized by an increasing use of metals for both tools and weapons.

Sumer. In about 5000 B.C. farmers settled on the fertile land of southern Mesopotamia (now Iraq) known as Sumer, eventually creating the world's first great civilization. By 3000 B.C. a number of city-states developed, the largest being Ur (population, about 40,000). Sumerian rule stretched from Syria to the Persian Gulf and lasted until about 2000 B.C.

Remembered for: First system of writing, wheeled vehicles, and a complex administrative and legal system.

Babylon. After 2000 B.C. the city of Babylon (south of present-day Baghdad) grew in strength, conquering Sumer and for the first time unifying the whole of Mesopotamia. Babylon was, in

---

THE WORSHIP OF JUST ONE GOD

Monotheism is thought to have emerged when the herdsman Abraham had a vision of the "one true God" in the early half of the second millennium B.C. The figure of Abraham is a shared spiritual ancestor in Judaism, Christianity, and Islam. In the Torah, Abraham is named as the ancestor of all Jews; in the New Testament, Jesus is descended from Abraham, the Father of Faith; and in Muslim tradition, Abraham (Ibrahim) is the Father of the Prophets and the ancestor of both the Jewish and Arabic peoples.

THE CODE OF HAMMURABI

From 1792 B.C. to 1750 B.C. Hammurabi ruled the vast Babylonian empire. His greatest legacy was a unified code of law—some 282 specific laws—that was used as a uniform code of justice throughout the empire. Although the laws were harsh by today's standards (famously, the principle of an eye for an eye and a tooth for a tooth), the code represented a huge step forward. Here was a justice system, uniformly applied, that guaranteed identical punishments for lawbreakers regardless of geography or status.

---

all likelihood, the first city to boast a population of over 200,000. In 539 B.C. Babylonia was invaded and fell to the Persians.

Remembered for: Code of Hammurabi and the beginnings of a rule of law.

Persia. In 550 B.C. Cyrus the Great conquered Assyria and became the first king of Persia. He went on to capture Babylon. By 486 B.C. Persia covered 2 million square miles, from northern India to the Mediterranean Sea, and extending through Turkey and Egypt. Defeat by the Greeks in the Persian Wars in the fifth century B.C. marked the beginning of its decline. In 330 B.C. Persia was conquered by Alexander the Great of Macedonia.

Remembered for: Largest empire ever, with an effective system of administration and taxes.

Other Early Civilizations

- **Minoans:** A trading and seafaring empire, centered on Crete and flourishing between 3000 B.C. and 1100 B.C., making it the earliest civilization of modern Europe.

- **Indus River Valley civilization:** Earliest recorded complex urban civilization on the Indian subcontinent (today modern Pakistan) from about 2500 B.C. to 1500 B.C. Developed urban planning, with straight streets and drains, as well as decorative stonework, irrigation, and a complex script.
- **Olmec civilization:** Centered on the Gulf of Mexico, this was thought to be the first civilization in Mesoamerica, coming to prominence around 1500 B.C.
- **Phoenicia:** Located in what is present-day Lebanon. Established naval city-states in the Mediterranean circa 1100 B.C. Developed a 22-letter alphabet, later adopted by the Greeks.
- **Hittites:** From about 2000 B.C. to 1190 B.C., the Hittites ruled over present-day Turkey in southwest Asia. Their military might was based on their ironworking skills.

Ancient Egypt

Ancient Egypt began with settlements along the banks of the Nile in northeastern Africa. By about 3200 B.C. the kingdoms of Egypt were unified in a single state 600 miles long. This was the beginning of a rich civilization that was to survive for 3,000 years, into the age of ancient Greece and Rome. Egypt's cultural and technological achievements were many, not least of which were the construction of monumental stone pyramids (tombs for their ruling families) and temples.

The history of Egypt is generally divided into the relatively stable periods of the Old, Middle, and New kingdoms, separated by periods of instability. The period known as the Old Kingdom (c. 2664–2155 B.C.) was ruled over by powerful

pharaohs and saw major developments in technology, art, and architecture. **Hieroglyphic script** was developed and **papyrus paper** invented. The vast **pyramids at Giza** (the lone survivors of the Seven Wonders of the World) were built at this time.

After a period of famine and strife, stability was once more restored when Mentuhotep II reunited Egypt. The Middle Kingdom lasted from about 2052 B.C. to 1786 B.C. Strong pharaohs reestablished control during the final Egyptian age of the New Kingdom (c. 1554–1075 B.C.), extending their influence into Syria, Nubia, and the Middle East. This is regarded as the greatest chapter of Egypt's history, during which many temples were built, including the painted tombs in the **Valley of the Kings.**

FAMOUS PHARAOHS

Hatshepsut: First female pharaoh

Tutankhamen: Boy king

Rameses II: Ruled for a remarkable 67 years

Cleopatra VII: Egypt's last pharaoh, the famous Cleopatra, ruled in the years leading up to Rome's conquest of Egypt in 30 B.C. In a quest for power, she allied herself first with Julius Caesar and then with Mark Antony.

After these three great ages, Egypt went into slow decline, though the influence of Egyptian culture was to be felt for hundreds of years. Over the following centuries, it faced successive invasions by the Libyans, Assyrians, and Persians. In 332 B.C. Alexander the Great conquered Egypt, which was then a Persian territory. **Alexandria** was established as the capital and a seat of learning at the mouth of the Nile.

Ancient Greece

Ancient Greece began as a loose association of **city-states** that were frequently at war and evolved into one of the greatest empires ever seen. The ancient Greeks made advances in philosophy, science, mathematics, art, trade, architecture, and literature, all of which profoundly influenced the Roman Empire, as well as all subsequent civilizations in the West.

The history of ancient Greece is often divided into four distinct periods: Archaic, Classical, Hellenistic, and Roman. It was during the Archaic period (c. 750–490 B.C.) that Athens,

THE GREEK PHILOSOPHERS HALL OF FAME

Two thousand years after the flowering of Greek culture, the writings of Greek philosophers are still being taught. The three philosophers who are always included in such studies are Socrates, Plato, and Aristotle.

- **Socrates:** Believed that there existed absolute truth and knowledge. He is also said to have taught that "the unexamined life is not worth living." Socrates was famous for his method of teaching using a question-and-answer approach, and Plato was his greatest student.
- **Plato:** Formed a school known as the Academy to further Socrates' teachings. Wrote *The Republic,* in which he set forth his vision of the perfect society.
- **Aristotle:** Came to Plato's Academy and stayed. He invented a method of arguing according to the laws of logic, which forms the basis of the scientific method. Aristotle's greatest student? Alexander the Great.

Sparta, Corinth, and Thebes emerged as the dominant city-states. The first **Olympic games** were held, **Homer** composed his epic *Iliad* and *Odyssey,* **Pythagoras** developed his theorem, and the Greeks established trading posts as far away as the Nile delta. Syracuse in Sicily and Byzantium on the Bosporus became major trading centers, and Greece as a whole prospered.

During the Classical era (c. 490–336 B.C.) the Greeks were united when they defeated the Persians, and the **Parthenon** was built in Athens in celebration. It was in this period that democracy became fully established under **Pericles,** the great tragedies of **Euripides** were written, and the philosophies of **Plato** and **Sophocles** developed.

ECHOES OF THE PAST

At his best, man is the noblest of all animals; separated from law and justice, he is the worst.

—Aristotle (384–322 B.C.)

The conquest of Greece in 338 B.C. by **Philip II of Macedonia** and the subsequent rule of Alexander III, better known as **Alexander the Great,** mark the beginning of the Hellenistic Period (c. 336–146 B.C.). During this time, the philosopher **Aristotle** (who also tutored Alexander the Great) composed much of his work. Greek culture and language were exported to the newly acquired Hellenistic kingdoms around the Mediterranean and Asia Minor. Alexandria in Egypt and Antioch in Syria became the new centers of Hellenistic culture, while the city-states of Greece declined in influence.

After the death of Alexander, the city-states secured some freedom for themselves, but it all came to an end in 146 B.C., when Greece was finally incorporated into the Roman Empire. Nonetheless, Greek ideas and culture permeated much of Roman society.

THE BIRTH OF DEMOCRACY

In the fifth century B.C., Athens successfully repulsed a Spartan invasion. In a bid to avoid tyrannical rule by local rich landowners, the people of Athens established the world's first democracy (from the Greek *demokratia*, "rule of the people"). All citizens had equal privileges, although non-citizens—slaves, females, and foreigners—had no rights at all.

The Roman Empire

The civilization of ancient Rome lasted for more than a thousand years, eventually encompassing most of western and northern Europe, North Africa, and the Middle East. As the Roman Empire spread over the globe, so did its language, art, technological innovations, and administrative systems. Eventually, the empire became hopelessly unwieldy and overstretched, making it vulnerable to attack from the fierce tribes of northern Europe.

Early Rome

Was Rome really founded by the twin brothers Romulus and Remus, the abandoned sons of the war god Mars, as legend has it? Historical sources say Rome began as a cluster of settlements on the seven hills beside the river Tiber, which joined together to form a city by 600 B.C. Rome was initially ruled by the **Etruscans,** rich traders from central Italy.

The Republic

In 509 B.C. Roman nobles drove out the seventh Etruscan king of Rome, Tarquin the Proud, and Rome became a republic, ruled by two consuls elected from the senate. Rome grew in strength, gradually overpowering everyone on the Italian peninsula, including the Etruscans and Greek settlers.

Roman expansion continued, and Rome clashed with Carthage in North Africa, leading to the **Punic Wars** (264–146 B.C.). It was during these wars that **Hannibal** famously marched his war elephants over the Alps,

ECHOES OF THE PAST

Courage is knowing what not to fear.

—Plato (429–347 B.C.)

ECHOES OF THE PAST

If it is not right, do not do it; if it is not true, do not say it.

—Marcus Aurelius (A.D. 121–180)

smashing the Roman legions at the Battle of Cannae in 216 B.C. By 146 B.C. Rome secured its first overseas possessions—Sicily, Spain, and North Africa; subsequent Macedonian wars left Rome dominant in Macedonia, Greece, and parts of Asia Minor.

Julius Caesar conquered Gaul (now France) in 51 B.C. and, after a period of civil war, appointed himself dictator for life. The senators responded by having him assassinated, leading to disorder and a struggle for dominance until Caesar's adopted son Octavian defeated **Mark Antony** and **Cleopatra** of Egypt at the Battle of Actium in 31 B.C. (when Egypt was also annexed). Octavian took the name Augustus, "the revered one," and became the first emperor of Rome in 27 B.C. Imperial rule continued for the next 400 years.

The Pax Romana

Augustus's reign spanned 41 years and brought with it peace and stability. While thousands of troops guarded the frontiers of the Roman Empire, Augustus continued to improve its infrastructure with the building of roads and great buildings.

The period from the rule of Augustus to the death of Marcus Aurelius in A.D. 180 is often called the Pax Romana (Roman peace), when the empire was relatively free from internal or external threat. Emperors from this period varied in capability and popularity. The most notorious were **Caligula,** who has been portrayed as insane and a sexual pervert, and **Nero,** the famous fiddler who ordered the burning of Christians.

ROMAN INNOVATIONS

- **Roads.** The Roman road system spanned more than 250,000 miles. Romans developed a form of concrete to produce a waterproof hard surface. Many of their typically straight routes form the basis of the roads in use today.
- **Architecture.** Roman architecture drew heavily from Greek styles, but the Romans' innovative use of arches and the invention of the dome became their hallmark. The invention of concrete allowed them to build more ambitious and durable structures, like the Colosseum.
- **Plumbing.** The Romans designed numerous aqueducts to feed the public water fountains where most people fetched their daily supplies. Large private houses, bathhouses, and public toilets eventually had indoor plumbing, using a network of lead pipes.
- **Heating.** The Romans developed underfloor heating, often used for bathhouses or opulent villas. The floor of a room would be raised on pillars so that hot air from a furnace could circulate in the hollow space and heat the room above.

The Decline of the Roman Empire

A series of incompetent and lesser-known emperors ruled after the Pax Romana, leading to a long period of imperial collapse. European and Asian enemies challenged Rome's power on many occasions, and the empire groaned under the weight of an unwieldy administrative system and an increasingly powerless army. In A.D. 286, Emperor Diocletian split the empire into eastern and western halves. Diocletian took charge of the eastern half and set up his government in Turkey,

and Maximian, the general in command of Gaul, took control of the western half.

In A.D. 324 Emperor Constantine I took command of the whole Roman Empire. He moved the capital to the Greek town of Byzantium, renaming it **Constantinople,** thereby establishing the **Byzantine Empire.** When Constantine's successor, Theodosius I, died in A.D. 395, the empire was again divided into east and west.

As the Byzantine Empire thrived in the east, the Western Roman Empire was increasingly weakened by battles with Germanic tribes and the so-called barbarian people to the north. In A.D. 406 the Rhine frontier was overrun, and Germanic tribes poured into the empire, finally sacking Rome itself in A.D. 455. In A.D. 476 the last Roman emperor, Romulus Augustus, was forced to abdicate, and the Western Roman Empire finally collapsed.

WHO WERE THE BARBARIANS AT THE GATE?

The last Roman emperor, Romulus Augustus, was overthrown in A.D. 476, but the fall of the Roman Empire was a process lasting many centuries, hastened along by waves of invading Germanic tribes who plundered cities and spread chaos through the region.

Vandals

Ostrogoths (Goths from the east)

Visigoths (Goths from the west)

Huns (led by Attila)

Lombards

Franks

Ancient China

Civilization in China emerged along the Yellow River in roughly the same time frame as in Mesopotamia. Evidence exists of the cultivation of silkworms as far back as 3000 B.C. By 2000 B.C. bronze working had begun.

Chinese tradition has it that the **Xia Dynasty** ruled in the Yellow River valley before the first recorded dynasty of the **Shang** took over, around 1600 B.C. The Shang followed a complex calendar, developed intricate jade carving, and made musical instruments. Writing emerged in 1200 B.C.

Following the Shang dynasty, the **Zhou dynasty** began its 900-year reign. (You may have been taught it was called the Chou dynasty.) The Zhou dynasty governed under a

> **ECHOES OF THE PAST**
>
> An oppressive government is more to be feared than a tiger.
>
> —Confucius (551–479 B.C.)

"mandate from heaven" and established a feudal system with a noble class controlling parts of the country. In this period, there were developments in agriculture, silk weaving, and the study of philosophy (most notably by **Confucius**). War craft advanced with the invention of the crossbow and the use of cavalry.

The **Qin dynasty** that followed lasted a mere decade (221–209 B.C.), but it had a profound impact. To keep out invaders from the north, separate fortification walls were joined, eventually becoming the **Great Wall of China.** During this time, laws, currencies, weights, and measures were all standardized, as was a system of writing.

The golden age of the **Han dynasty** lasted for four centuries (206 B.C.–A.D. 220). During this period, Confucianism became the state doctrine. China had contact with the West via the Silk Road, which brought **Buddhism** to China. Other Han dynasty accomplishments included a civil service based on competitive exams, the invention of a seismograph to detect earthquakes, accurate clocks, the use of iron plows pulled by oxen, and burning coal to smelt iron. Paper made from wood pulp and probably gunpowder were invented at this time. Han scientists invented the rudder for use on ships, and they created other useful devices, such as the fishing reel and the wheelbarrow. Han artists and architects are noted for their detailed carvings in jade, wood, or ivory and the building of elaborate temples.

BEGINNINGS OF BUDDHISM

Siddhartha Gautama was a prince who lived near the present-day border of India and Nepal more than 2,500 years ago. Raised in great luxury, the prince wanted to understand what caused human suffering. He left his home, gave up his possessions, and lived the life of an ascetic, praying and fasting in a quest for enlightenment. Eventually, enlightenment came, along with the understanding that all life is suffering.

Siddhartha became well known for his teaching. His students called him "the Buddha," which means "the Enlightened One," and the followers of Siddhartha's teachings are called Buddhists. The Buddha taught his followers to seek balance in their lives. The path to happiness is neither through indulgence nor denial, but through the Middle Way. Siddhartha taught that by putting aside your ego, you can escape the cycle of death and rebirth to reach Nirvana.

The Four Noble Truths

1. Life means suffering.
2. The origin of suffering is attachment.
3. The end of suffering is attainable.
4. The path to the end of suffering is the Middle Way between self-denial and desire.

Ancient India

Around 1500 B.C. light-skinned migrants came to the Indus River valley from Europe. They developed a caste system that segregated Brahmans (priests) from warriors and from peasants or traders. Eventually a fourth caste of craftsmen was formed. The caste system proved enduring as it grew more complex and rigid. (The caste system was finally abolished by the Indian constitution in 1949.)

Over the next several centuries, until 250 B.C., the Aryans migrated south and continued to push their influence across the Indian subcontinent.

Golden Age of India

The **Gupta empire** included most of the Indian subcontinent and oversaw a very peaceful and prosperous period from about A.D. 320 to A.D. 550. Called the Golden Age of India, it was marked by extensive inventions and advances in science, technology, engineering, mathematics, and astronomy. **Hinduism** emerged during this period, and classic works of art and literature reflecting both Hinduism and Buddhism were created. It is also thought that the board game of chess was invented.

Mayan Civilization

From about 300 B.C. to A.D. 850, the Mayan civilization dominated what is now southern Mexico and parts of Central America. As in ancient Greece, the Mayans were organized into city-states (but were ultimately ruled by one king). Like the Egyptians, the Mayans built pyramids.

Without horses, oxen, or other large animals, the Mayans relied on human labor for building their cities and producing the corn and cotton upon which the cities depended. Wars to capture slaves for labor were common.

The golden age of the Mayans lasted from about A.D. 500 to A.D. 850. During that time, they developed a complex system of measuring time via the Mayan calendar as well as an understanding of astronomy. They also figured out how to grow corn, beans, squash, and cassava on marginal land, build elaborate buildings and cities, and communicate via one the world's first written languages. Various theories have been proposed for the decline of Mayans, many of which center on the idea of agricultural decline from drought, deforestation, and unsustainable agricultural practices.

Come on,
it's not *that* dark

Chapter 2

A Dark Age in Europe; Golden Ages to the East and West

As the Roman Empire weakened, a great movement of Germanic tribes overran Europe in search of land and new settlements, leading to the collapse of the Western Roman Empire. New kingdoms arose, including the Frankish nation, whose powerful leaders successfully fought off Arab invasion and extended the influence of Christianity in Europe. Some history books refer to this period as the Dark Ages because much of the language and culture of classical antiquity disappeared and few records of the period survive.

Meanwhile, outside Europe, the Byzantine Empire thrived, the golden age of Islam preserved much of Western culture, and China experienced dazzling cultural advancements during the Tang dynasty.

Byzantine Empire

Constantinople (now called Istanbul) was the capital of the Byzantine Empire. Built by the Roman emperor Constantine (A.D. 285–357), it was a new city, where Greek and Roman culture was preserved and treasures from all over the empire adorned its new buildings. Constantine was the first Christian emperor; he reversed the anti-Christian laws of Emperor Diocletian, promoted religious tolerance, and made Christianity the official religion of Constantinople.

Constantinople became the hub of a major trading network that extended across Europe, Asia, and North Africa, and the city itself became famous for its wealth, art, and architecture. From A.D. 527 Christian emperor Justinian I further expanded the empire by conquering North Africa and parts of Italy. By his death, in 565, the Byzantine Empire stretched from Spain to Persia.

The Rise of Islam

Around A.D. 610 **Muhammad,** an Arab merchant, had a vision in which he was instructed to preach a new faith centered on one true God, Allah. As he delivered his message, he attracted many adherents, and the new faith of Islam (meaning "submission to the will of God") spread throughout Arabia. Between the seventh and eighth centuries Islamic rule expanded rapidly under the Umayyad caliphates (ruling dynasties) to become one of the largest empires in history. It

ISLAM AS RELIGION AND A WAY OF LIFE

The central tenet of Islam is that there is only one God: Allah. To be a Muslim, a believer must carry out five duties that demonstrate the Muslim's submission to the will of God. These five duties are known as the Five Pillars of Islam:

- **Faith.** The central belief is expressed as "There is no God but Allah, and Muhammad is the messenger of Allah."
- **Prayer.** Muslims pray five times a day, facing Mecca. They may pray in a mosque, but it is not necessary. In any Muslim town five times a day, the Muslim call to prayer is sounded throughout the town. It begins with "Allah u Akbar," which means "God is Great."
- **Alms.** Muslims are required to support those less fortunate than themselves.
- **Fasting.** During the Islamic holy month of Ramadan, Muslims neither eat nor drink between dawn and sunset to remind themselves that they have spiritual needs as well as physical ones.
- **Pilgrimage**. All Muslims are required to make a pilgrimage to Mecca at least once in a lifetime.

Muslims believe that Moses and Jesus had both existed and that both were holy men, as was Muhammed. Many of the stories in the Qur'an (Koran) are the same as the stories in the Judeo-Christian Bible. Muslims believe that the Qur'an perfects the earlier revelations that make up the Jewish Torah and the Christian New Testament.

---

was at this time that Islam split into two camps—the **Shia** and the **Sunnis**—based on conflicting views of who was the rightful heir to Muhammad.

The Arabic Islamic empire encroached upon the Christian Byzantine Empire and eventually stretched from the borders of China to North Africa and into the Iberian Peninsula. With the ascension of the Abbasid Caliphate in A.D. 750, the golden age of Islam began, with a capital in Baghdad. Lasting until the thirteenth century, this period witnessed a revitalization of scholarly and religious thought—resulting in major developments in agriculture, the arts, sciences, law, medicine, mathematics, industry, economics, and literature—and preserved the classical writings of ancient Greece and Rome.

In the mid-eleventh century a wandering group of Muslim Turks took over the Abbasid lands, captured Byzantium in 1071, established their own ruling dynasty, and then settled in large numbers across Asia Minor (thereby precipitating the Crusades). The Turkish language and Islam replaced Christianity in much of the region.

Holy Roman Empire

Meanwhile, back in the West, a Germanic tribe known as the Franks dominated much of western Europe. In A.D. 732 the Frankish king Charles Martel fought off the invasion of Arab forces at Poitiers, thereby preventing Arab domination in western Europe. Martel's grandson **Charlemagne** ruled over the Frankish empire (also called the Carolingian empire), which eventually covered France, part of Spain and Germany, and much of Italy.

Charlemagne (meaning Charles the Great) instigated a 30-year campaign to conquer and Christianize Europe. Having supported Popes Hadrian I and later Leo III in ridding Italy of the Lombards, he was invited to Rome and crowned Holy Roman emperor on Christmas Day A.D. 800. Made up of a union of central European territories, the Holy

Roman Empire was a key driving force behind the Crusades and lasted for more than a thousand years, with Napoleon bringing it to an end in 1806.

East-West Schism

In the eighth and ninth centuries, increasing theological and political differences between Constantinople and Rome led to the permanent division of the Christian church in Europe, known as the East-West Schism. In 1054 Constantinople broke with the church in Rome to form the **Eastern Orthodox Church.** As a result, Russia and eastern Europe followed a different cultural path than western Europe, which continued to follow the authority of the pope.

Beginnings of England and France

The Angles, Saxons, and Jutes were Germanic-speaking peoples who invaded and settled in Britain between the fifth and seventh centuries. Their migration from Germany and the Jutland peninsula (present-day Denmark) was part of the general movement of Germanic people throughout Europe at this time. By A.D. 600 the southern and eastern parts of England were established as Anglo-Saxon kingdoms.

The Normans were descendants of Vikings (their name is derived from Norsemen), as well as the Franks and Romans who had settled in northern France. They frequently gave shelter to the Vikings after their raids on Britain and other areas of western Europe. In order to prevent this, the English king Ethelred II (nicknamed Ethelred the Unready) made a treaty with the Duke of Normandy, in which each promised not to aid the other's enemies. Ten years later he consolidated

THE VIKINGS: RAIDERS AND TRADERS

Between the eighth and eleventh centuries, Vikings from areas now known as Denmark, Sweden, and Norway attacked the coastlines of Europe, rowing inland along the Loire, Rhine, and other rivers. They traveled as far as Russia from the Baltic and threatened Constantinople, sailing vast distances to "raid and trade" and making the first-known voyages to Iceland, Greenland, and North America.

---

the pact by marrying the duke's sister, Emma, in 1002. Thus began the association of Normandy with England.

By the time of Ethelred's death in 1016, there was dissent and confusion in England, and the Viking king Canute seized the throne. Following the reigns of Canute's sons Harold Harefoot and Hardecanute, the throne returned to Saxon rule under Edward the Confessor in 1043. Edward returned from exile in Normandy, where he had befriended many Norman nobles, including William, Duke of Normandy (known in the future as William the Conqueror).

The Battle of Hastings

When King Edward died in 1066 without an heir, several contenders, including William of Normandy, stepped forward to claim the throne. William and the powerful English lord Harold Godwinson each claimed that Edward had named *him* as the heir.

Harold was crowned, but the battle for the throne continued until the Battle of Hastings, in September 1066. Harold died on the battlefield—the scene is gruesomely depicted in the Bayeux Tapestry, which shows an arrow piercing his eye. William the Conqueror was crowned William I, king of England, at Westminster Abbey on Christmas Day 1066. The Normans went on to conquer Wales, some of Ireland, parts of Scotland, southern Italy, and Sicily.

From this point on, the Normans and their descendants replaced the Anglo-Saxons as the ruling class of England. Closely aligned with France, the early Norman kings and nobility held land on both sides of the English Channel and were predominantly French-speaking. As time progressed, however, the distinction between Norman and English blurred, so that by the 1300s, the Norman aristocracy thought of themselves as English.

China and Japan Flourish

Europe may have been experiencing a "dark age," but that wasn't the case in China. After the collapse of the Han dynasty in A.D. 220, nomadic people from the steppes and Tibet

INVENTIONS OF THE TANG AND SONG DYNASTIES

The Tang and Song dynasties brought tremendous growth, prosperity, and innovation to China. The impact of many of the innovations of this period rippled across the world, changing the course of history.

- **Mechanical clocks.** Clocks in China in the 700s were driven by water power. The idea was carried to medieval Europe. By the 1300s, Europe had developed clocks powered by weights.
- **Porcelain.** Developed in the late 700s, this bone-hard white ceramic became a valuable export for China. The secret to making "china" was kept for centuries.
- **Printing.** Block printing, in which one block is cut for an entire page, was developed in the 700s. In 1040 movable type was invented. Printing spread to Korea, Japan, and later Europe.
- **Gunpowder.** Explosive powder made from a mixture of saltpeter, sulfur, and charcoal was developed in the 800s and first used for fireworks. Later it was developed into weapons. The Arabs acquired knowledge of gunpowder sometime between 1240 and 1280, and the technology spread to Europe shortly thereafter.
- **Paper money.** The Song Dynasty introduced paper money in 1020 to help out merchants.
- **Magnetic compass.** A floating magnetized needle that always pointed north helped make China a sea power in the 1100s. The technology soon spread west.

---

conquered much of northern China. Some 30 local dynasties rose. Finally, the short-lived Sui dynasty united China, only to fall to the Tang.

The Tang dynasty (A.D. 618–907) was one of China's golden ages. China greatly expanded its territory beyond its current borders. Trade stretched to Southeast Asia, and the religion of Buddhism spread to Korea and Japan. At the same time, Confucianism again rose as a semireligious instrument of the state.

After the decline of the Tang dynasty, China experienced a short period of general chaos, with no strong, central government. In A.D. 960 the first Song emperor reunited most of China. Under the Song, China began rice cultivation, planting two crops a year, which resulted in surplus food. As a result, there was a flourishing of art and literature. Song artisans were known for their landscape paintings, fine porcelain, and the use of calligraphy, a form of fine handwriting. The Song also developed paper money and maintained extensive trade with India, Persia, and the Middle East. The Song dynasty lasted until 1279.

Japan Borrows from China

For a long time the 4,000 islands that make up Japan were controlled by various clans. China's influence started to be felt in the sixth century, and the Japanese adapted the Chinese system of writing, styles of art, tea drinking, and Buddhism.

In A.D. 794 Japan established a capital in Heian (present-day Kyoto) and became less interested in China as a cultural influence. Feudalism was pervasive during the Heian period (until 1185), and warlords maintained armies of samurai. In the late 1100s one family became the most powerful ruling clan, and the emperor gave the clan the title of **shogun.** The shogun's headquarters was in Kamakura, and the period became known as the Kamakura shogunate. A pattern of weak emperors backed by powerful shoguns continued in Japan until 1868.

Chapter 3

The Middle Ages

The political and economic system of feudalism is thought to have emerged as a stabilizing influence in Europe after the collapse of the Roman Empire. Feudal relationships could be complex and sometimes ambiguous, but contractual obligations based around the tenure of land and the provision of military service were the building blocks of medieval society in Europe.

Kings leased lands known as fiefs to powerful lords or vassals in return for their allegiance and homage. The lords then divided their lands into manors or estates, which they leased to lesser nobles or knights. Similarly, religious institutions might own estates for which tenants or lesser nobles were obliged to pay homage. At the very bottom of the social heap was a class of unfree peasants (villeins, or serfs) who lived—and died—under the jurisdiction of the lord.

The Middle Ages included a terrible pandemic, huge social change, rebellion, and religious conflict that rumbles on to this day. The Black Death wiped out nearly a third of the population of Europe and in the process sowed the seeds for social change. The Middle East became a battleground between Christian and Muslim empires, and new ideas and goods were exchanged along with bloody blows. Meanwhile, the Mongols conquered much of Asia and left a lasting legacy.

The Crusades

In 1095 Pope Urban II, in response to a plea for help from the Christian Byzantines, who were under attack from Muslim Turks (see page 32), called upon the nobility of western Europe to come to their defense in the First Crusade. This was the beginning of almost two centuries of military campaigns in the Middle East.

The aim of the Crusades was to recapture the Christian Holy Land—Syria and Palestine—from its Islamic rulers. The Crusades were frequently marked by their brutality and increasingly fought as much for commercial gain as spiritual salvation. Despite almost 200 years of sporadic conflict, most of Palestine remained in Muslim hands.

A MEDIEVAL MANOR

At the head of a typical estate or manor stood a nobleman with land set aside for himself (usually the bigger part) and the rest divided into small holdings to lease to his tenants, who were obliged to work the nobleman's land in addition to their own. A holding was a share (usually a strip) of a large unfenced field. Each field would contain a different crop to form part of a simple rotation. In addition, there would be common land where tenants could graze livestock.

The estate was a self-sufficient unit where everything produced was for consumption and nothing was for sale. After a bad harvest, or in times of scarcity, locals had to depend heavily on their lord's provisions—or starve.

MEDIEVAL CHIVALRY

A distinctive code of conduct emerged from the privileged position of being a mounted knight or "chevalier" (from which we get the word chivalry). Knights were expected to be honorable, courageous, loyal to the king, courteous—especially toward women—and generous.

Although there are no documents that set out a specific code of chivalry, it was documented in an epic poem called *The Song of Roland,* which is also the oldest piece of French literature in existence. Written between 1098 and 1100, *The Song of Roland* describes the code of conduct of the eighth-century knights who fought with Emperor Charlemagne. The idea of chivalry is further expressed in legends of King Arthur and the Knights of the Round Table. Arthur's legacy as a leader in the late fifth and early sixth century was firmly established when it was set down by Geoffrey of Monmouth in *Historia Regum Britanniae* (History of the Kings of Britain), written in 1138.

Commercial Gains of the Crusades

Trade flourished throughout the Middle East and Europe during the Crusades, and the Crusaders were accompanied by a retinue of clerics, scholars, and merchants—all of whom had their own interests. Exotic Middle Eastern goods, such as lemons, dates, sugar, coffee, diamonds, cotton, gunpowder, writing paper, mirrors, and carpets, were introduced to Europe. New scientific ideas and inventions, such as Arabic numerical figures, algebra, waterwheels, clocks, chemistry, and irrigation, were also introduced.

The Crusaders were not averse to occasional plundering, and the British Museum, the Louvre, and other European institutions still house treasures and relics brought back from the Crusades.

THE KNIGHTS TEMPLAR AND THE KNIGHTS OF MALTA

The Knights Templar were an international religious military order founded in about 1120 by a band of knights who vowed to protect Christian pilgrims traveling to the Holy Land. In battle they wore characteristic white robes with red crosses.

The Knights Hospitallers were another Christian military order, and in 1070 they ran a hospital for sick pilgrims in Jerusalem, with Muslim permission. From 1530 they were known as the Knights of Malta, having been given the island of Malta by Holy Roman Emperor Charles V. Malta was strategically important for trade as well as pilgrimage (and for that reason would be later occupied by the French and the British, before being granted independence in 1964). Both orders attracted noble members and grew immensely wealthy and powerful.

Magna Carta

Richard I, the Crusader king, was succeeded by his brother John, an unpopular ruler who lost vast territories in France and continually squeezed his unhappy subjects with higher and higher taxes to pay for his military humiliations overseas. By 1215 his barons had had enough and forced him to sign the Magna Carta (the Great Charter), a document limiting the king's powers.

The Magna Carta is arguably Britain's most famous legal document. However, in spite of its fame, only three of its 63 clauses are still recognized by English law. One of these guarantees the rights of individual subjects, leading some to claim that the Magna Carta was a proclamation of the rights of common men, though in reality it was drawn up to protect the interests of the wealthy few.

Black Death

The Black Death swept through Europe and the Middle East in the mid-fourteenth century and was the most virulent and terrifying form of bubonic and pneumonic plague ever recorded. It is thought to have killed about a third of the total European population— about 25 million people—by the time it died out in 1351.

The origins of the plague are uncertain, but it is believed to have started in the 1330s in the Far East by germ-bearing fleas carried on rodents. From China (where it is said to have killed 13 million people) it rapidly spread westward along the Silk Road. It then hit the Byzantine Empire with devastating ferocity (in Constantinople they called it the Great Dying). By 1348 it had reached cities in France, Spain, and England. A year later it had spread to Germany, Russia, Scandinavia, and then parts of the Middle East.

The first signs of Black Death were a high fever and black swellings or hard pus-filled boils, appearing first on the armpits, groin, and neck, and then all over the body. Most people who were infected died within 48 hours. The clothes of the dead were burned, and bodies were taken away by cart and buried in a deep pit. There was no cure and no preventive treatment.

Hundred Years' War

England had controlled a large amount of land in France since the reign of William I, and there was continual friction between the two nations over territories. After Philip IV of France confiscated Aquitaine in 1337, Edward III of England responded by claiming the French crown, thus setting off a series of wars that would last 116 years and bankrupt the English crown. At the outset the English were victorious, and Edward defeated Philip at Crécy in 1346. He was aided by his son, also Edward, dubbed the Black Prince for the color of his armor. Land was gradually lost to the French under the leadership of a new king, Charles V.

In the fifteenth century, war was declared once more, by Henry V (portrayed so memorably in Shakespeare's eponymous play), who renewed the English claim to the French throne. In 1415 he invaded France and famously defeated the French at the Battle of Agincourt.

After Henry's sudden death on campaign, possibly of dysentery, his brother John, Duke of Bedford, acted as regent in France for Henry's young son Henry VI. Bedford had several successes until **Joan of Arc** led the French to victory in 1429. Over the next few years England lost the majority of its French territories, culminating in 1453 when Bordeaux was recaptured by the French and only Calais was left under English rule.

Peasants' Revolt

When Edward III died, his grandson Richard II came to the throne at just eleven years old. For the next few years England was effectively ruled in his stead by his uncle John of Gaunt. John, a son of Edward III, had fought under his father in the Hundred Years' War.

John was an unpopular figure, widely blamed for losses of French territories during the Hundred Years' War and for the crippling taxes needed to finance them. This, combined with dissatisfaction with the oppressive feudal system, pushed the peasantry to desperate measures.

Rioting over taxation culminated in the Peasants' Revolt in 1381. The revolt ultimately failed, but it was the first mass uprising of common men, and a sign that the old social order was changing.

Vast Mongol Empire

The Mongols were nomadic warring tribes from Inner Asia. In the twelfth century a charismatic leader arose who united (or conquered) all of the tribes and earned the title **Genghis Khan** (ruler of the world).

By about 1250 the Mongol Empire included three semi-independent realms: China and Mongolia, Persia, and Russia (the Khanate of the Golden Horde). Although in theory they were subject to the khan in Mongolia, in practice the realms were fully independent. In 1255 the Mongol rulers of Persia went to war against the Abbasid caliph, invading Syria and Palestine. In 1258 they captured Baghdad, snuffing out the intellectual flowering of Islam.

The westward advance of the Mongols was halted at one of the decisive battlefields of history: Ayn Jalut, near Nazareth in Israel, in 1260. Here Turkish and Egyptian forces routed the Mongols, preventing an attack on Egypt and North Africa.

In 1260, the grandson of Genghis Khan, **Kublai Khan,** ascended the throne. Between 1267 and 1279 the Mongols completed the final conquest of China, but they were unable to extend their reach to Japan, Southeast Asia, and Indonesia. In 1271 Kublai Khan formally established the **Yuan dynasty** with Yuandadu (currently Beijing) as the capital.

By the 1300s the entire length of the **Silk Road** was under the control of a vast Mongol Empire that extended from China to eastern Europe. This facilitated the free passage of Mongolian armies, traders, and other travelers, who inadvertently hastened the spread of the Black Death. The total area of the country was over 4.6 million square miles. Its crowning

MARCO POLO

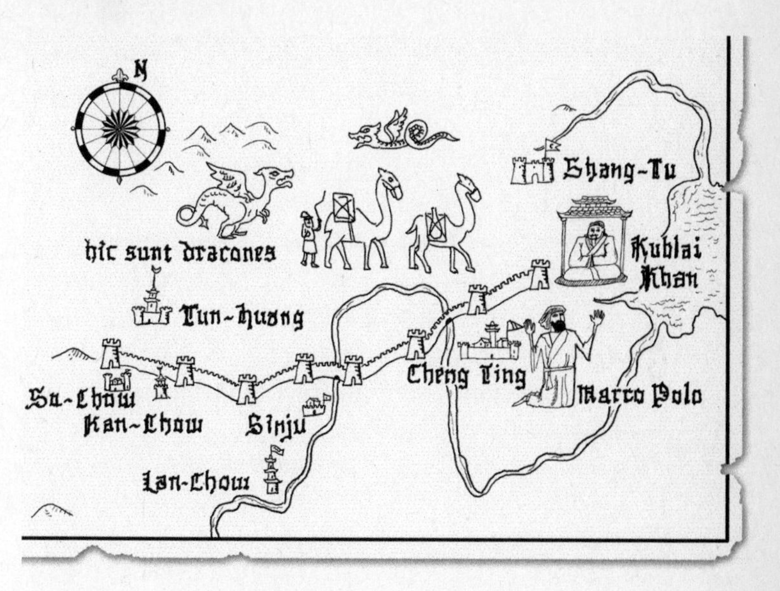

Marco Polo was, perhaps, the most famous visitor to China during the Yuan dynasty, though the records show that numerous other traders and diplomatic emissaries also visited China at this time. Polo's best-selling book told Europeans about a culture far more advanced than anything they could imagine. He described stones used for fuel (coal) and cloth that would not burn (asbestos). Most unbelievable, he claimed to have seen country after country, with China at the far end, bigger than Europe, with larger and cleaner cities, ships more impressive than anything in Europe, and money made of paper.

achievement was the building of the **Forbidden City,** where all future Chinese emperors lived.

The Decline of the Mongol Empire

The Yuan dynasty lasted only 98 years, but the cat was out of the bag. As a result of European contact with China during this period, Europe now had gunpowder, the compass, and the concept of the printing press.

Peasant revolts in China toppled the Mongol government, and the Ming dynasty took its place. China expelled all foreigners and closed its borders in 1368.

As Mongol power declined in the Middle East, new principalities were created in Byzantium. One principality created by Osman I gradually expanded into the Ottoman Empire.

The Mongols remained in power in central Asia and Russia.

The Aztecs and Incas in the Americas

The Aztecs rose to power in the mid-1200s and built their capital at Tenochtitlan, which is now Mexico City. Like the ancient Romans, the Aztecs were warriors who conquered vast territories and linked them together with roads. They allowed self-governance in the conquered territories, as long as tributes and taxes were paid regularly to the king. Like the Mayans, the Aztecs required human resources for building, but they also required huge numbers of people each year for sacrifices to the gods.

Like the Aztecs, the Incas were also expansionist and warlike. In the 1400s the Incas conquered an empire that stretched along the Pacific Coast of South America. They instituted a strong central government and controlled their empire through the use of an elaborate road system. These roads linked the empire together using a system of relay runners. Incans excelled at engineering and built complex stone structures without mortar. Incan engineers also developed improved methods of terrace farming.

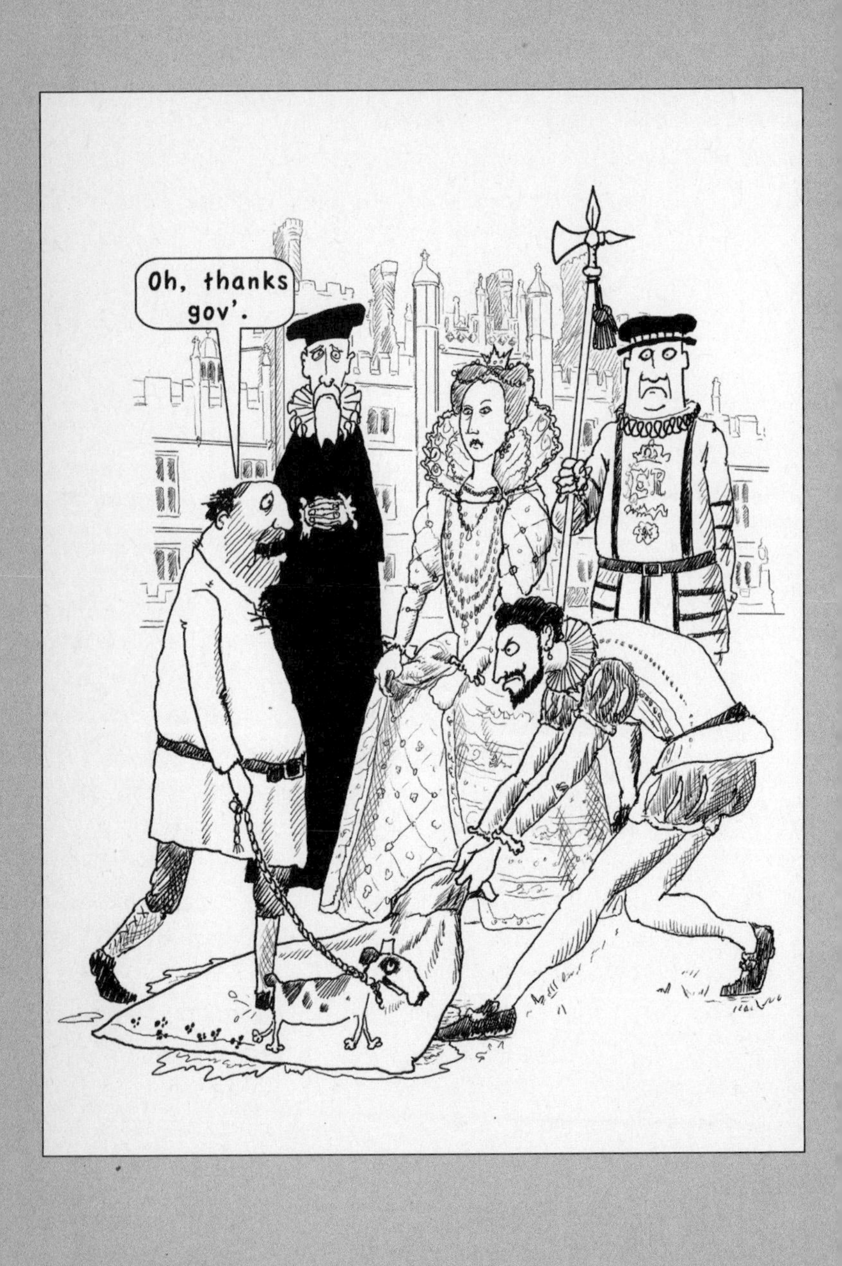
Oh, thanks gov'.

Chapter 4

Renaissance, Reformation, and Religion

Important changes occurred during the Middle Ages that led directly to the Renaissance and Reformation. Agriculture became more reliant on horsepower over oxen power, and farming became more efficient. The Crusades brought about an explosion in trade and a desire for goods from the Near and Far East. As a result of both factors, towns and cities grew.

With the growth of a money-based economy rather than a land-based economy, wealthy nobles began to demand that they pay soldiers to do their fighting for them rather than having to fight themselves. Meanwhile, the merchants and craftsmen of medieval towns organized into guilds, a different form of governance.

The fifteenth and sixteenth centuries were a time of momentous change across Europe as scholars, artists, and philosophers rediscovered classical texts, art, and ideals. The quest for knowledge threw new light on established ideas about Church and state, leading to the religious upheaval of the Reformation and the spread of radical Protestantism in northern Europe. In the Middle East and India, Islam spread as new empires arose.

Renaissance

The Renaissance (meaning "rebirth") was an artistic and intellectual reawakening that originated in Italy in the fourteenth century and spread to the rest of Europe. A renewed interest in the culture and values of ancient Greece and Rome led to an embrace of **humanism,** a school of thought that placed greater importance on the abilities of the individual rather than on the divine or supernatural. Scholars, clerics, writers, and artists all drew on and expanded classical themes in their quest for knowledge and improvement. There are too many Renaissance luminaries to list in full, but here are a few creative souls who pushed the boundaries of their disciplines:

Francesco Petrarch (1304–1374): Italian poet and scholar, Petrarch is regarded as the Father of the Renaissance and one of the earliest humanists. He was instrumental in collecting and preserving classical Greek and Roman texts.

Filippo Brunelleschi (1377–1446): The foremost architect and engineer of the Italian Renaissance, who designed the huge dome, or *duomo,* of Santa Maria del Fiore in Florence and was greatly influenced by Greek and Roman styles.

Sandro Botticelli (1444–1510): Working mainly in Florence under the patronage of Lorenzo de' Medici, Botticelli was inspired by the legends of ancient Greece and Rome. His most famous paintings include *The Birth of Venus* and *Primavera*

(Spring). He also helped decorate the Sistine Chapel in the Vatican.

Lorenzo de' Medici (1449–1492): The Medicis were a fantastically rich Florentine banking family. Lorenzo, like his grandfather Cosimo, was a generous patron of the arts who funded, nurtured, and welcomed into his court many of the key artists of the Renaissance period, including Botticelli and Michelangelo.

Leonardo da Vinci (1452–1519): A renowned artist and master of a dizzying array of disciplines. Leonardo's best-known work of art is the *Mona Lisa*. He was also a sculptor, a pioneer of anatomy, an inventor, an architect, and an engineer.

Desiderius Erasmus (1466–1536): The Dutch scholar Erasmus formed the new Christian humanism, studying the original Greek New Testament, questioning the Church and rejecting the notion of predestination. In 1509 he wrote *In Praise of Folly*, criticizing the abuses of the church and raising questions that would be influential in the Protestant Reformation.

Niccolò Machiavelli (1469–1527): This Florentine philosopher and statesman wrote *The Prince*, which examined how states should be governed and advised that the effective use of power may necessitate the use of unethical methods.

ECHOES OF THE PAST

In her [Nature's] inventions nothing is lacking, and nothing is superfluous.

—Leonardo da Vinci (1452–1519)

ECHOES OF THE PAST

In the country of the blind the one-eyed man is king.

—Erasmus (1466–1536)

Some have accused him of atheism and cynicism, and his name has become synonymous with ruthlessness and cunning.

Michelangelo di Buonarroti (1475–1564): One of the great artists of the Renaissance, Michelangelo created two of the frescoes in the Sistine Chapel. He was also an architect and a sculptor, best known for his *Pietà* in St. Peter's Basilica in Rome and the exquisite *David* commissioned for the Cathedral of Florence.

THE INVENTION OF THE PRINTING PRESS

The invention of the mechanical printing press by German metalworker **Johannes Gutenberg** in 1440 may have been the most crucial development of the Renaissance. Before this, books were laboriously copied by hand. With a mechanical press, books could be produced in multiple copies and widely owned. Gutenberg's press changed the course of the political world, the religious world, scholarship, and eventually, everyday life. His printing techniques quickly spread across Europe and were crucial to the free circulation of ideas.

Reformation Shakes Up the Church

The Reformation was a movement born from a widespread discontent with the power and corruption of the Catholic Church. It had its roots in the Renaissance, when scholars

like Erasmus questioned the doctrines and practices of the Church, and when new translations of the Bible provoked fresh debates about Catholic doctrines. The ideas of the Reformation spread throughout northern Europe, causing Protestantism to take root in the north, while Catholicism remained entrenched in the south.

Martin Luther triggered the Reformation when he nailed 95 theses to a church door in Wittenberg in 1517. An Augustine monk and a professor of biblical studies at Wittenberg University, Luther was protesting the excesses and hypocrisy of the Catholic Church. His criticisms of the Church and his determination to question and reform its practices sparked the Protestant revolution in Germany. Luther went on to

THE INQUISITION

Special tribunals, appointed to root out and punish heresy, had been a feature of the Catholic Church since the Middle Ages, but the most notorious was the Spanish Inquisition, set up in 1478 by Pope Sixtus IV, under pressure from Ferdinand and Isabella of Spain. Though Catholicism remained entrenched in southern Europe, the Reformation shook the papacy enough for the Inquisition to persecute Protestants, as well as Jews, Muslims, and other heretics. Who were the heretics? Original thinkers like the astronomer Galileo, who was summoned by the Roman Inquisition in 1616 for arguing that the Earth revolves around the sun. Many of those tried had their land or possessions confiscated or were tortured or burned alive. The Inquisition was finally abolished in 1834.

---

translate the Bible into German and to attack the central Catholic doctrines of transubstantiation (the conversion of the bread and wine of the Eucharist into the body and blood of Christ), clerical celibacy, and papal supremacy.

Aided by the invention of **Gutenberg's** printing presses, Luther's ideas swept through Germany and Europe. The English Protestant **William Tyndale** translated the New Testament into vernacular English in 1526 but was captured and executed for heresy in the Low Countries before he could complete his translation of the Old Testament. By 1530 Sweden, Denmark, and parts of Germany were receptive to Luther's reforms and proceeded to break with the Catholic Church.

One of the key moments in the Reformation occurred when **Henry VIII** of England broke with Rome in 1534 and formed the **Church of England,** which his daughter **Elizabeth I** formalized. In so doing they laid the foundations of an institution that would survive centuries of religious quarreling.

John Calvin

John Calvin became the second-greatest reformer after Luther, although they disagreed on some points. Under Calvin's leadership, Protestantism became the dominant religion in Switzerland. It was Calvin's vision of doctrinal revolution, later known as **Calvinism,** that became the driving force behind Protestantism in western Germany, France, the Netherlands, and Scotland.

Elizabeth I: The Virgin Queen

Daughter of Henry VIII and Anne Boleyn, Elizabeth took the throne in 1558 after the death of her half-sister, the fiercely Catholic Mary I, and English Protestants rejoiced.

On her accession, Elizabeth swiftly set about reconciling a nation divided by religion. She picked her way through politics carefully, and after much wrangling, her first Parliament passed two great acts that solidified the newly formed Church of England. The Act of Supremacy reestablished the monarch as the head of the Church, and the Act of Uniformity instituted the second prayerbook of her half-brother Edward VI. Her aim was to introduce a moderate form of Protestantism that would appeal to English Protes-

ECHOES OF THE PAST

Come live with me and be my love,
And we will all the pleasures prove,
That valleys, groves, hills, and fields,
Woods, or steepy mountain yields.

—Christopher Marlowe (1564–1593)

ECHOES OF THE PAST

What a piece of work is a man,
how noble in reason, how infinite
in faculties, in form and moving
how express and admirable,
in action how like an angel, in
apprehension how like a god!

—William Shakespeare (1564–1616)

tants without offending Catholics too greatly.

The Elizabethan Golden Age

Arts and culture flourished during Elizabeth's reign. Poets such as **Edmund Spenser** composed great works of literature; public theaters, such as the Globe, were built under the patronage of various nobles; and dramatists such as **Ben Jonson** and **Christopher Marlowe** wrote plays that endure to this day. The most important writer of the period was **William Shakespeare** (1564–1616), whose prolific career outlasted Elizabeth; between 1590 and 1613 he wrote 154 sonnets and at least 38 plays, which are still performed today.

THE SCIENTIFIC REVOLUTION

While Europe was awakening to the arts, an equally important scientific awakening was occurring, begun by **Copernicus** (1473–1543) and **Galileo** (1564–1642), whose observations led them to conclude that the Earth revolved around the sun. **Francis Bacon** (1561–1630) asserted that science must be based on observation and mathematics. **Johannes Kepler** (1571–1630) developed the laws of planetary motion, and **Isaac Newton** developed his theory of gravity and invented calculus to prove it.

All of this scientific development had a profound impact. First, it challenged the absolute authority of the Church. Second, it laid the groundwork for the Industrial Revolution.

Spread of Islam

The years between 1300 and 1700 were a time of expansion for the Muslim world. The Byzantine Empire was fading, and the Seljuk Turk state had been destroyed by the Mongols. Islamic empires were established in the Middle East and India.

The Ottoman Empire

Anatolia (Turkey) was inhabited by groups of nomadic Turks, including one that was led by Osman I. These Turks were called Ottomans, and by 1326, under Osman's leadership, they set up a new empire with a capital in Istanbul. Leaders called themselves sultans, or "ones with power." They extended the kingdom by forming alliances when they could and conquering when they had to. The military success of the Ottomans was aided by gunpowder—especially as used in cannons.

In 1514 the Ottomans took Persia, Syria, and Palestine. Next they captured Arabia, with the Muslim holy cities of Medina and Mecca, and gained control of Egypt.

Suleiman I, who came to the throne in 1520, brought the Ottoman Empire to its greatest size and most impressive achievements. He conquered parts of southeastern Europe by 1525. He won control of the entire eastern Mediterranean Sea and took North Africa as far west as Tripoli. Although he was defeated in a battle for Vienna in 1529, his Ottoman Empire remained huge. The empire lasted long after Suleiman but spent the next few hundred years in decline. None of the sultans were as accomplished as he had been, and the Ottoman Empire's power slipped.

Persia

Farther to the east the **Safavids,** practitioners of Shia Islam, built up a strong army to protect themselves from their Sunni neighbors. In 1499 a 14-year-old leader named Ismail led this army to conquer Iran. He took the traditional Persian title of shah, made the new empire a Shia state, and killed off Baghdad's Sunni population. Ottoman Turk rulers—who were Sunni Muslims—in turn killed all the Shia that they met. This conflict between the two groups of Muslims continues today.

The Safavids reached their height in the late 1500s under Shah Abbas. During this time, rug making, which had simply been a local craft in Persia, was changed into a major industry for the country. As with the Ottoman Empire, the Safavid empire began to decline soon after it had reached its greatest height.

The Mughal Empire in India

In 1494, at the age of 14, a Muslim by the name of Babur inherited a small kingdom north of present-day India. He raised an army and set out to conquer Samarkand, Kabul, and other parts of central Asia and India. He is known as the founder of the Mughal Empire, so called because his family was related to the Mongols. Although Babur's son lost most of the empire, his grandson, Akbar, won it back.

Akbar was a Muslim, but he believed strongly in religious tolerance. During Akbar's reign, many changes in culture took place. His policy of blending different cultures produced two new languages. Hindi blended Persian and local languages. It is still widely spoken in India today. Urdu grew out of a mixture of Arabic, Persian, and Hindi and was spoken by the soldiers in Akbar's camp. Today it is the official language of Pakistan. Art flourished in the Mughal Empire, especially book illustrations and architecture.

After Akbar's death in 1605, the empire began to decline. The most famous emperor to follow was Shah Jahan. He chose not to follow Akbar's policy of religious toleration but was a great patron of the arts, building many beautiful buildings, including the famous **Taj Mahal.**

Don't look now, it's Columbus again. Give him a few boats and tell him to clear off.

Chapter 5

The Age of Discovery

The sixteenth century saw the beginning of the great age of European exploration. Sparked in part by the exchange of cultures that took place during the Crusades, Europeans now looked beyond the edge of the known world and wondered what other lands were yet to be discovered. New shipbuilding technology, better navigation techniques, and the development of cartography meant that European sailors could travel farther than ever before. The expanding Ottoman Empire in the east also spurred European commercial expeditions to find new sea trade routes to circumvent the Ottomans in the west. Command of the sea now played an increasing role in the power balance between European nations.

Portuguese and Spanish Exploration

With its extensive coastline and position at the southwestern tip of Europe, Portugal had long been a seafaring nation. Throughout the fifteenth century, expeditions led by **Prince Henry the Navigator** explored the coast of Africa as the Portuguese began to look for sea routes to Asia where they could trade gold, silver, spices, and other goods. By the late fifteenth century, Spain had also joined the search for new trade routes.

In the sixteenth century Portugal went on to establish a string of trading posts, from the coasts of Africa and Brazil to China. The Spanish also firmly established themselves in the West Indies and Central and South America, colonizing by force in Mexico and Peru, among other New World colonies. By the end of the sixteenth century, Spain's conquests overseas had made it the richest nation in Europe.

Explorers Hall of Fame

Driven by a desire for wealth and converts to Christianity, explorers set off into the unknown. The successful ones are remembered today:

- **Vasco da Gama:** Found a sea route to the East Indies via the Cape of Good Hope (thus avoiding Ottoman-controlled territories on land) in 1498.
- **Amerigo Vespucci:** Between 1499 and 1502 the Italian navigator, in the service of the king of Portugal, made several voyages to the New World, during which he claimed to have been the first to sight South America.

SOUTH AMERICAN CIVILIZATIONS

From the beginning of the sixteenth century, the native cultures of South America were disrupted by European colonies; first by the Portuguese, who landed and colonized Brazil in 1500 and then by the Spanish, who claimed much of the continent. In 1520 Spanish soldier Hernan Cortés seized Mexico, despite fierce resistance, and slaughtered and enslaved many Aztecs in the process. The Incan empire was similarly brought to an end when Spanish conquistador Francisco Pizarro landed on the coast in 1532, killing its emperor Atahualpa (but only after he had paid a huge ransom to the Spaniards).

- **Christopher Columbus:** With the support of the Spanish crown, this Italian set off across the Atlantic, reaching the Caribbean and finally central and southern America in later voyages.
- **Ferdinand Magellan:** Under the Spanish flag the Portuguese explorer discovered a route to circumnavigate the globe in 1520.

English Adventurers

Early English attempts at exploration were sparked by **John Cabot** (an Italian navigator sailing under the English flag), who landed on the island of Newfoundland in 1497. In 1562 it was decided that England should also venture into the New World and see what it had to offer. Elizabeth gave sanction to the privateers John Hawkins and **Francis Drake** to engage in the work of slave trading by abducting slaves from West African towns and Spanish and Portuguese ships and transporting them to sell to colonists in the West Indies. Elizabeth later gave her blessing to piratical raids against foreign treasure ships returning from the New World, further antagonizing Spain.

From the late 1570s the idea that England should attempt to establish its own empire to rival those of Spain and Portugal became more widespread. A colony on the coast of present-day North Carolina was named Virginia in honor of Queen Elizabeth, but a lack of supplies and foresight on the part of the settlers caused the colony to fail. Virginia was not fully established until the following century, but by 1670 there were British settlements in New England, Virginia, Antigua, Barbados, Jamaica, and Honduras, with the East India Company trading from 1600. The Hudson's Bay Company was founded in 1670 and established itself in Canada.

Other Early Empires

During the 1600s the Dutch empire established itself as a significant naval and economic power. Founding the Dutch East India Company in 1602, it gradually overtook Portugal in the silk and spice trade, seizing various trading posts from the Portuguese in the East Indies and Asia. The Dutch also colonized Mauritius in 1638; in 1652 Portugal established a settlement at Cape Town, South Africa (a useful outpost for the route to Asia), before setting up colonies in the West Indies and, briefly, in Brazil. France also acquired most of its colonial empire in the 1600s, including substantial territories in North America and Canada, the Caribbean, and India. To a lesser extent, the Swedes temporarily secured outposts on the Gold Coast of Africa, and Denmark, in unison with Norway, also established a few trading settlements on the Gold Coast, as well as in the Caribbean and India.

The Defeat of the Spanish Armada

From the moment Elizabeth ascended the throne, war with Spain was an ever-present threat. She managed to postpone its outbreak for 30 years, but by 1587 Philip II of Spain had had enough of Elizabeth's raids on Spanish ships and her support of Protestant rebels in the Spanish-controlled Netherlands. He planned to invade England with a vast fleet of ships, but a surprise raid, led by **Sir Francis Drake,** on the assembling fleet set back the Spanish plans for a year.

The Spanish Armada, consisting of about 130 heavily laden ships, finally set sail in July 1588. It was met by about a hundred English ships led by Drake and Lord Howard of Effingham. The English ships were smaller, faster, and better armed, and they hounded the Spanish as they sailed up the

English Channel, forcing them to seek shelter in the port of Calais. In the night, the English sent eight blazing ships crashing into the enemy fleet, driving the Spaniards out into the North Sea. Subsequently, much of the Spanish fleet was lost or shipwrecked in violent North Atlantic gales.

More than 60 ships are recorded to have made it back to Spain, and perhaps 15,000 Spanish sailors lost their lives, while the English lost only a handful in battle. Though it was the bad weather that ultimately trumped the invasion, the defeat of the Spanish Armada has been celebrated as one of the greatest English victories.

Seeking Religious Freedom

Many Europeans settled in the New World in the hope they could practice their religion without fear of persecution, some belonging to religious sects formed during the turmoil of the Protestant Reformation.

In September 1620 about a hundred colonists—the Pilgrims—set sail from Plymouth to North America on the *Mayflower.* Many of them were fleeing religious persecution in England, and about a third were Separatist Puritans who had originally immigrated to the Netherlands but now wished to settle in America. The London Virginia Company, which had established the first English colony at Jamestown in 1607, gave them a license to settle in the colony of Virginia. However, rough seas pushed the *Mayflower* off course and she landed farther north, at Cape Cod. The settlers who survived the voyage established a settlement at New Plymouth, in present-day Massachusetts.

THE COLUMBIAN EXCHANGE

The Columbian Exchange refers to the exchange of diseases, ideas, food crops, and populations between the New World and the Old World following the voyage to the Americas by Christopher Columbus in 1492. Its importance cannot be overemphasized.

The gold and silver found in the New World was an immediate attraction for Europe, but the discovery of new food staples, such as potatoes, sweet potatoes, corn, and cassava had greater long-term impact. Also new to the Old World were tomatoes, chile peppers, cacao, peanuts, and pineapples. Tobacco, another New World crop, was so universally adopted that it came to be used as a substitute for currency in many parts of the world.

Europeans brought deadly viruses and bacteria, such as smallpox, measles, typhus, and cholera, for which Native Americans had no immunity. On their return home, European sailors brought syphilis to Europe.

Dutch Calvinists founded New Amsterdam, which later became New York. They also settled in South Africa, where they became known as the Boers. French Huguenots settled in North America and the Cape of Good Hope. British Quakers settled in Pennsylvania, along with Baptists and German and Swiss Protestants. Spanish and Portuguese Jews settled in Dutch Brazil in the 1650s but fled to North America when it was taken over by the Portuguese, joining other Jews fleeing persecution in Europe, who then established communities around New York and Rhode Island.

China and Japan Prefer Isolation

From 1500 to about 1800, European trading posts were established in many port cities, but European influence was not spreading so rapidly in Asia. Japan and China both felt the spread of Christianity was a threat to their power. They already practiced their own religions, specifically Hinduism, Buddhism, Shintoism, and Confucianism.

China

The Ming dynasty (1368–1644) succeeded in driving out the Mongols and reuniting the country. It put strict controls on traders and heavily taxed the manufactured goods the traders sought. The Qing dynasty (1644–1912) continued the trade policy of the Ming dynasty, requiring tributes from foreign traders.

Japan

The strong Tokugawa shogunate took power in Japan in 1600 after a period of chaos known as the Warring States period. The Europeans brought firearms, which had a profound impact on the samurai culture. They also brought Christianity, which the rulers considered disruptive. In 1639 Japan closed its borders and instituted a "closed country" policy that would last 200 years.

Some people aren't taking this seriously.

Chapter 6

The Age of Reason and Revolution

The seventeenth and eighteenth centuries were characterized by clashes of ideology: between monarch and parliament, state and the individual, and across the religious divide between Protestants and Catholics. In Britain bitter civil war ultimately led to drastic constitutional overhaul, while later revolutions in America and France resulted in the creation of the United States of America and the French Republic. Revolutionary ideals in both nations were, in part, fed by the eighteenth-century school of thought known as the Enlightenment, which championed reason and the rights of the individual. At the same time, the global economy was invigorated by agricultural and industrial revolutions, which gathered pace first in Britain and then across the rest of the world.

The Enlightenment

The Enlightenment, or Age of Reason, was a cultural and philosophical movement underpinned by a belief in the power of reason. Beginning in the seventeenth century, it gained momentum during the eighteenth century as Enlightenment thinkers questioned established institutions and the accepted social order and attacked both superstition and the Church itself as an enemy of reason. As a movement, it championed secular values and paved the way for the democracy and liberal capitalism of modern society. Its theories were to influence science, politics, law, economics and the arts, and it formed the intellectual basis for the French and American revolutions.

Writers and philosophers, such as **Voltaire** and **Jean-Jacques Rousseau** in France, began to apply Enlightenment principles to society, making the case that all people are equal. In Britain the philosophers **Adam Smith** and **David Hume** advocated empiricism and economic liberalism, social reformer **Jeremy Bentham** argued for the abolition of slavery, and the political writer **Thomas Paine** wrote in support of American independence and French revolution.

Civil War in England

In England the only son of the Catholic Mary Queen of Scots, James Stuart, succeeded the childless Elizabeth I in 1603 as James I. James was a Protestant, and like Elizabeth, he had

SCIENTIFIC REVOLUTION

In the Age of Reason, scientists came to believe that observation and experimentation would allow them to discover the laws of nature, reflecting a shift from belief in the dogma of the Church to a belief in empiricism. The scientific method as a means of proving hypotheses emerged, but the method required tools. Soon the microscope, thermometer, sextant, slide rule, and other instruments were invented.

Scientists working during this time included **Sir Isaac Newton** (gravity and theories of motion), **Joseph Priestley** (isolated and described oxygen and carbon dioxide; invented soda water), **Benjamin Franklin** (electricity), and **René Descartes** (analytic geometry; "I think, therefore I am").

Scientists and mathematicians made rapid advances in astronomy, anatomy, mathematics, and physics. The advances had an impact on education: Universities introduced science courses to the curricula, and elementary and secondary schools followed suit. As people became trained in science, new technologies emerged in the form of complicated farm machinery and new equipment for textile manufacturing and transportation, paving the way for the Industrial Revolution.

---

sought to keep the peace between Protestants and Catholics during his reign as James VI in Scotland. Upon taking power, James immediately made peace with Spain, and for the first half of the seventeenth century, England remained largely inactive in European politics.

Within England, however, James was a contentious figure because of his uncompromising belief in the divine right of kings. Such absolutism led him into conflict with anyone who questioned his authority, particularly with Calvinist Protestants who believed in a more contractual form of monarchy. James argued that the king should pass the laws and control Parliament, not the other way around.

During this time, radical (or, as they were dubbed at the time, "hot") Protestants, or Puritans, questioned the current translations of the Bible and the ceremonies of the Elizabethan Church. James took the opportunity to commission a new translation of the Bible, but with all the revolutionary and antimonarchical references removed. Completed in 1611, the King James Bible has endured for centuries.

On the death of James I in 1625, his son Charles I came to the throne. Like his father, Charles believed in the divine right of kings. This, combined with his determination to strengthen Catholic traditions in the Anglican Church, brought him into conflict with his Parliament. This led to a civil war that drew in all sectors of society, with communities and families divided by conflicting allegiances. Finally, in 1649, a republic (or what some would call a military dictatorship) was established, with Oliver Cromwell at the head, and Charles I was executed. Cromwell's rule came to be known as the Commonwealth. Following his death in 1658, Cromwell's son Richard became Lord Protector, the highest position in the land.

The Restoration

Richard Cromwell failed to control either the army or Parliament; after eight months he was forced to abdicate. A group of army officers and members of Parliament invited Charles I's son, Charles Stuart, back from exile in France and installed him as King Charles II in 1660, marking the beginning of the Restoration period.

THE THIRTY YEARS' WAR (1618–1648)

Fought mainly in Germany, the Thirty Years' War was sparked by a revolt in Bohemia against the Habsburg Holy Roman emperor Ferdinand II. The war quickly drew in other nations, including Denmark and Sweden, and became a struggle for power in Europe. In 1635 France entered the fray, fearful of Habsburg domination. Peace was concluded in the **Treaty of Westphalia** in 1648, although the Franco-Spanish War continued until 1659. France became the dominant power in Europe, and the Holy Roman Empire lost importance within the context of Austrian and Prussian rivalries.

The monarchy was restored with much public jubilation—its popularity a reaction in part to the strictly Puritanical regime that had been imposed during the Commonwealth, when fines were given out to people for gambling and drinking, and holidays such as Christmas and Easter (thought to be pagan in origin) were suppressed. By contrast, the "Merrie Monarch" was a fun-loving king who reopened the theaters and encouraged science, art, music, and dancing.

The Glorious Revolution

When Charles II died in 1685 with no legitimate heir, his Catholic brother James succeeded him as James II, to the consternation of the largely Protestant Parliament. Revolution was set in motion when James II fathered a son in 1688, making the threat of a Catholic dynasty a reality.

Already troubled by the king's Catholicism and his alliance with France, leading politicians of both the Whig and Tory parties invited Charles II's Protestant daughter Mary and

THE BRITISH BILL OF RIGHTS (1689)

The Bill of Rights is one of the most important documents in British history and was the precursor to the U.S. Bill of Rights and influenced later constitutional law around the world. It laid out certain basic rights of all Englishmen living under a constitutional monarchy. These included freedom from royal interference with the law, freedom from taxation by Royal Prerogative, and freedom of speech and debates. As a prelude to the 1701 Act of Settlement, the Bill of Rights also stipulated that Roman Catholics should be excluded from the crown.

---

her husband, William of Orange, to England. William and Mary deposed James II and were crowned joint monarchs in 1689. Parliament affirmed its authority with the Bill of Rights, a document that established England as a **constitutional monarchy.** With no living offspring, the crown then passed to Mary's younger sister Anne.

The Acts of Union

Queen Anne became the last of the Stuart monarchs in 1702. When it became apparent she would leave no male heir, a crisis over succession led to the Act of Settlement in 1701, which barred Catholics—and anyone who might marry a Catholic—from the throne. Perhaps the most important legacy of Anne's rule was the Acts of Union in 1707, which merged England and Scotland as one sovereign state, in the phrase of the Acts as "one united kingdom by the name of Great Britain." In 1801 the second Act of Union (partly provoked by the Irish Rebellion of 1798) proclaimed the United Kingdom of Great Britain and Ireland.

THE WAR OF THE SPANISH SUCCESSION (1701–1713)

The War of the Spanish Succession was a conflict that arose following the death of the Spanish Habsburg king, Charles II. With no natural heir, he bequeathed his territories to Philip, Duc d'Anjou, who also happened to be in line to the French throne. The terrible prospect of a union between France and Spain caused shock waves across Europe, and in a bid to prevent it, an alliance was formed in 1701 between the English, the Dutch, and most of the German princes in support of an Austrian claim to the Spanish empire.

Fighting took place mainly in Europe but also in North America, where the English fought against the French in Queen Anne's War between 1702 and 1713. The war ended with the Treaty of Utrecht in 1713, which recognized Philip of Anjou as Philip V of Spain but removed him from the French line of succession. Britain emerged more powerful, gaining considerable territory in North America, as well as the right to ship slaves to the Spanish colonies.

The American War of Independence

Relations between Britain and its American colonies deteriorated during the eighteenth century, largely because of colonial resentment at the commercial policies of Britain and lack of representation at Westminster. A conflict over taxation culminated in the Boston Tea Party in 1773, when protesting colonists dumped three shiploads of tea into Boston Harbor. Protest developed into armed resistance at Concord and Lexington in 1775 and finally full-scale war. King George III refused to compromise over taxes or address the colonists' grievances, and public sentiment favored

independence (partly fueled by Thomas Paine's pamphlet "Common Sense"). With no hope of a peaceful resolution, the Second Continental Congress drew up the **Declaration of Independence** on July 4, 1776.

The declaration gave moral justification for the war with Britain and unified the American colonies under one cause. But Britain was not prepared to concede without a fight, and the war continued for another five years. Despite outnumbering the rebels, Britain suffered from problems of supply (each soldier required a third of a ton of food to be transported

ECHOES OF THE PAST

We hold these truths to be self-evident, that all men are created equal, that they are endowed by their Creator with certain unalienable Rights, that among these are Life, Liberty and the pursuit of Happiness.

—Declaration of Independence (1776)

THE SHOT HEARD ROUND THE WORLD

In 1837 American essayist and poet Ralph Waldo Emerson wrote "Concord Hymn," celebrating the American Revolutionary War. In it he referred to the opening battle of the war as "the shot heard round the world." There is some historical truth to the sentiment, because the American Revolutionary War had a great impact on the rest of the world, especially in inspiring the French Revolution. Later, however, the phrase was put to use in Europe to refer to the shot that killed Archduke Franz Ferdinand and plunged Europe into World War I.

every year), a hostile population, lack of local knowledge, and the guerrilla tactics of the colonists.

In 1778 the Continental Congress formed an alliance with France. Over the next two years Spain and the Dutch Republic also declared war on Britain, during which British forces were distracted by conflict in Minorca and Gibraltar and in the East and West Indies. A Franco-American force won the final major battle at Yorktown, Virginia, in 1781. After two years of negotiation, the 1783 **Treaty of Paris** finally concluded Britain's capitulation and recognized the independence of the United States of America.

The War of 1812

Some 30 years after the War of Independence, hostilities between Britain and the United States broke out once more, due to trade blockades between France and America during the Napoleonic Wars (see pages 94–96). Britain also began seizing thousands of sailors from American merchant ships in the Atlantic for enlistment into the British navy.

War was declared in June 1812. American warships won a series of engagements but were unable to break up the British blockade. There were a series of large, inconclusive battles across America, the most famous being the British raids on Chesapeake Bay that resulted in the burning of the president's mansion in Washington, D.C. (known as the White House from 1901).

When Britain defeated France in the Napoleonic Wars, trade restrictions were lifted and the two sides signed a peace treaty in Belgium on Christmas Eve 1814 (though news did not reach America until February 1815, by which time the Americans had defeated the British at New Orleans).

The French Revolution

The French Revolution changed the face of Europe as monarchy and the established order of the ancien régime were swept away in favor of a government based on the Enlightenment principles of citizenship and equality. It was also one of the most violent and bloody chapters in France's history.

France had been gripped by a financial crisis caused by Louis XVI's involvement in the Seven Years' War (see page 84) and his support of the colonists in the American War of

ABOLITION OF THE FRENCH MONARCHY

In 1792 war with Austria led to a series of French Revolutionary Wars (see page 94) and brought more radical policies. The king and his Austrian queen, Marie Antoinette, were suspected of backing an Austrian victory. The monarchy was abolished and the king and queen tried and executed in 1793.

Independence. High bread prices and unemployment led to hunger and crippling poverty among much of the population, who resented the privileges and ostentatious consumption of the nobility. In May 1789 the financial crisis led to the calling of the Estates-General, a representative assembly organized into three estates: the church, the nobility, and the Third Estate (everybody else). When it became clear that the clergy and nobility could outvote the Third Estate, its bourgeois leaders began a struggle for equal rights.

In June 1789 the Third Estate reconvened and declared itself the National Assembly, an assembly of the "people," not of the estates. The monarchy and nobility attempted to dissolve the National Assembly, which was prevented by the sansculottes—the artisans and workers of Paris, who rose up and attacked the Bastille on July 14. The king consequently lost

---

THE SEVEN YEARS' WAR (1756–1763)

The Seven Years' War drew in all the major powers of Europe and involved two linked conflicts: the struggle for supremacy in Germany between Austria and Prussia and colonial rivalry between Britain and France. Prussia fought mainly on European soil against the combined forces of Russia, France, Austria, and Sweden, while its ally Britain clashed with France over colonial territories in North America, Africa, and India. The Treaties of Paris and Hubertusburg concluded the war in 1763. Their terms reduced France's imperial influence, increased Prussia's status within central Europe, and established British as the leading colonial power, gaining India and North America, including French Canada.

---

control of Paris and the countryside when a series of peasant rebellions, known as the Great Fear, took hold over much of France in a summer of panic between July and August 1789.

The National Assembly then passed the August Decrees, abolishing noble privilege, and published the Declaration of the Rights of Man and of the Citizen, a proclamation of human rights and civic equality modeled on the Declaration of Independence of the United States.

Between 1789 and 1791 the Constituent Assembly proceeded to implement a number of radical reforms. These included legislation that radically limited the power of the Catholic Church in France, abolishing its rights to impose tithes, appropriating its property, dissolving religious orders, and severing its ties with the pope. The church was made a wing of the state. For the first time counterrevolution received mass support and the king fled to Varennes as demands for a republic were voiced.

THE IRISH REBELLION OF 1798

Roused in part by the success of the American and French revolutions, a group called the United Irishmen staged an uprising in 1798, with the aim of securing independence from England. The rebellion, which became a popular one against landlords and Protestants, ultimately failed—in spite of military assistance from revolutionary France—and was brutally quashed by the British army. The conflict was marked by its violence and ferocity, involving massacres, torture, and rape, and leaving between 30,000 and 40,000 Irish dead.

While France suffered from high inflation, revolts, and defeat by the Austrians, the National Convention, which had been elected to provide a new constitution, set up the Revolutionary Tribunal and the Committee of Public Safety, which became dominated by the more radical Jacobins and their leader **Maximilien Robespierre.** The committee implemented the Great Terror between September 1793 and July 1794 to crush any resistance to the regime. Robespierre, its key driving force, called it "*justice implacable.*" Real or imagined enemies of the regime were executed, and it is estimated that around fifty thousand people died (most of them peasants or urban workers) either on the guillotine, in counterrevolutionary clashes, or in jail.

Dissent grew among the Jacobins, and Robespierre, along with twelve others, was sent to the guillotine without trial in July 1794, bringing an end to the Terror. There were several different forms of administration before the coup d'état of Brumaire in 1799, which then established the consulate of Napoleon Bonaparte (see page 95).

IVAN THE TERRIBLE; PETER THE GREAT

Ivan III liberated Russia from the Mongols, but Ivan IV was a terror. His reign started well enough in 1547, with the establishment of a Russian code of rules, but ended with secret police and a reign of terror. Peter the Great took the throne in 1696 (he shared the throne with his half brother Ivan V from 1682 to 1696) and did much to modernize and reform Russia.

Culturally isolated by the Mongols, and geographically isolated as well, Russia had missed out on the Renaissance and the age of exploration. Peter modernized the army, created a navy, established contact with western Europe, and gained access to the Baltic Sea and Baltic trade as a result of the Northern War with Sweden (1700–1721). Peter the Great moved the Russian capital to St. Petersburg and proclaimed himself emperor. By the time of his death in 1725, Russia was a power to be reckoned with.

The Agricultural and Industrial Revolutions

In Britain a revolution was set in motion during the latter half of the 1700s, spurred less by bloodshed and war than by economic and social forces. It transformed a mostly rural society into a modern, urbanized, industrial power. The effects of the agricultural and industrial revolutions later spread across Europe and America, causing enormous social change and economic growth, along with the rise of a powerful new middle class.

The Agricultural Revolution

For many centuries, British farmers had farmed their land on narrow strips in open fields belonging to wealthy landowners. But in the 1700s, landowners began taking over the strips to make larger, more productive fields, with some landowners also taking over common land. Government legislation, culminating in the General Enclosure Act of 1801, led to large-scale reform resulting in the enclosure of a quarter of England's farmland. As enclosed fields were grouped together to form larger farms, many rural workers and smaller landlords were forced to seek employment elsewhere.

Key Developments of the Agricultural Revolution

At the same time that land holdings were being consolidated, new technology was changing agriculture and making it more efficient.

- **The four-field crop rotation system:** A Dutch system introduced in the 1730s improved productivity. Instead of having fields left fallow every third year in order to rest the soil, crops like turnips or clover that improved the fertility of the soil were grown, providing winter food for livestock.
- **The seed drill:** A mechanical seeder developed by Jethro Tull in 1701 carefully planted seeds into the soil instead of scattering them across the surface by hand, ensuring a better rate of germination and a higher crop yield.
- **Selective breeding:** Robert Bakewell and Thomas Coke began to select the healthiest, most productive animals from which to breed and experimented by combining different breeds, resulting in an increase in market value of livestock and greater yields.

The Industrial Revolution

As farming methods improved and overseas trade grew, Britain's manufacturing also underwent a major transition from one based on manual labor to a mechanized one. A stable government, the availability of capital, as well as crucial reserves of coal and iron ore all ensured that Britain was at the forefront of the Industrial Revolution, but it soon spread to Europe and America in the nineteenth century.

Key Developments of the Industrial Revolution

There were a number of new inventions that sped up production. A few of these included:

- **The flying shuttle:** Patented in 1733, it enabled a single weaver to throw the shuttle across the loom and back again with one hand.
- **The spinning jenny:** This new spinning machine enabled operators to spin eight threads at once.
- **Water power:** In 1769 Richard Arkwright designed a water-powered spinning machine. In 1785 Edmund Cartwright made the first water-powered loom, which was later driven by steam.
- **Sheet iron:** In 1709 Abraham Darby worked out how to produce sheet iron from coke (a pure form of coal), resulting in the large-scale production of iron goods. Most industrial machines, steam engines, and later the railroads were all made from iron.
- **The steam engine:** The industrial steam engine was improved and developed by James Watt. By 1800 there were more than 500 of Watt's engines in Britain's mines, mills, and factories. His engine made possible the construction of new factories that could run year-round away from water sources.

Transformation of Europe

The Industrial Revolution caused a rise in large-scale factories and increasing urbanization as traditional craftsmen, laborers, and their families migrated from rural areas to the growing towns and cities in search of work. Industrial workers generally earned a tiny wage, and conditions in many of the factory towns were grim—inadequate housing and poor sanitation often led to the spread of disease. Child labor was common, with children expected to work up to 16 hours a day operating dangerous machinery. Factory reforms later improved working conditions and legislated against the use of child labor.

In the nineteenth century, industrialization spread to Europe—first to Belgium, and then on to the larger countries of the continent. New coalfields facilitated the expansion of the railroads. After unification in 1871, industry spread rapidly in Germany, particularly in the steel, chemical, and electrical industries. At the same time, industrialization increased exponentially in the United States, aided by its vast railroad network and iron- and steelmaking industries. By 1900 the United States was the world's biggest industrial power.

The New Age of Transport

The process of industrialization went hand-in-hand with improvements to the transport system. Raw goods and finished products needed to be transported, and new developments in materials and engineering enabled thousands of miles of roads, canals, and railroad tracks to be built.

- **Roads:** From around 1720, newly established turnpike trusts in Britain built and maintained thousands of miles of new roads, for which they collected a toll at gatehouses built at either end of the road (many of which can still be seen today). The Scotsman John McAdam invented a process for building harder, more weatherproof roads using a layer of small stones coated with tar (called tarmacadam or tarmac in his honor).
- **Water transport:** Robert Fulton's steam-powered boat took its first voyage in 1807. In England and the United States, a vast network of canals linked manufacturing centers with rivers and ocean harbors for transport. In the United States, extensive canal systems were built in Lowell, Massachusetts, considered to be "the Cradle of the American Industrial Revolution." Canals were also built

in Lawrence, Massachusetts; Holyoke, Massachusetts; Manchester, New Hampshire; and Augusta, Georgia.

- **Railroads:** In 1804 Richard Trevithick produced the first steam-powered engine. George Stephenson then improved the design with the "Rocket" steam locomotive and was responsible for the world's first passenger steam railroad, built in 1825. Construction of public railroads linking cities with towns began in the 1830s. By 1855 thousands of miles of railroad tracks snaked across Britain. Thereafter, railroads were built across the world with the United States completing the first transcontinental railroad, linking the Atlantic with the Pacific in 1869. By the end of the century, railroad networks reached across Europe, the United States, Canada, and some parts of Russia.

Chapter 7

The Age of Empire

The Industrial Revolution led to further advances in technology and science as well as a period of expansionism as European nations looked overseas for raw materials to feed their rapidly growing industry. Europeans also believed that they should spread Christianity throughout the world. Revolutionary France pursued an aggressive expansionist policy under Napoleon. At the same time, the newly independent United States extended farther west toward the Pacific, and European powers carved up a great mass of colonies overseas, with Britain, in particular, building a vast empire. The popular saying, "The sun never sets on the British Empire" was more true than not. Britain controlled Australia, India, parts of Africa, and the vast lands of Canada in North America.

European nations fought near-constant colonial conflicts, and the newly unified empire of Germany emerged as a major power in Europe. The resulting tensions would later erupt into World War I.

The French Revolutionary and Napoleonic Wars

In Europe a series of wars raged in the late eighteenth and early nineteenth centuries as various European coalitions fought against the French. First were the French Revolutionary Wars (1792–1802), when Austria, Britain, Prussia, and others sought to restore Louis XVI to power. This was followed by the Napoleonic Wars (1803–1815) to limit the aggressive expansion of **Napoleon Bonaparte.** Both wars raged throughout Europe but were also fought in the Middle East, southern Africa, and the Caribbean, as the French gained and then lost a vast empire.

Napoleon secured a series of decisive victories against the Austrians in northern Italy in 1796, but his fleet suffered defeat by the English under Admiral **Horatio Nelson** in Egypt in 1798. The British and French signed a peace agreement at Amiens in 1802. Britain renewed the war a year later, in response to Napoleon's occupation of Malta. In 1805, Nelson destroyed the combined Spanish and French fleet at the Battle of Trafalgar, during which he was mortally wounded. In the same year, Napoleon defeated the emperors of Austria and Russia at the Battle of Austerlitz. Victory in the Napoleonic Wars led to the expansion of French influence throughout much of western Europe (excluding Britain) and into Poland.

Napoleon next set his sights on Spain, but his invasion of the Iberian Peninsula was repelled by Spain, Portugal, and Britain during the Peninsular War in 1811. Napoleon's

NAPOLEON BONAPARTE (1769–1821)

One of the greatest military leaders in history, Napoleon began his career at the age of 14, took over the leadership of France in the military coup of 1799, and by 1804 was named the emperor of the French. Napoleon's troops conquered Austria, Prussia, Spain, Portugal, and kingdoms within Italy. By 1810 his empire was at its greatest extent, but it lasted only five years. Conflicts with Britain, nationalist uprisings in Italy, and guerrilla warfare in Spain and Portugal undermined his power.

The Battle of Waterloo ended Napoleon's time in power, and he died in imprisonment. In the end, his **Napoleonic Code** (1804), which recognized the equality of French (male) citizens, was his greatest legacy.

Moscow campaign in 1812 was an even worse disaster. His army was decimated by a bitter Russian winter and the Russian scorched-earth policy, leading to the death of nearly half a million men (the retreat was commemorated by **Tchaikovsky** in his *1812 Overture*). After another defeat for the French at Leipzig, the Duke of Wellington invaded France in 1814. Napoleon was forced to abdicate and was imprisoned on the island of Elba.

Napoleon escaped from Elba in 1815 and retook power in France for a brief period known as the Hundred Days, but was finally defeated by Wellington, aided by the Prussians, at the **Battle of Waterloo.** Napoleon was banished well out of harm's way to St. Helena

ECHOES OF THE PAST

An army marches on its stomach.

—Napoleon Bonaparte (1769–1821)

in the South Atlantic, and Britain emerged as a leading world power and mistress of the seas.

The British Empire

The British Empire reached its peak during the Victorian era, covering, at its greatest extent, one quarter of the world's landmass—the largest empire ever known. Britain's new technology, prosperity, and shipbuilding skills—as well as the commercial force behind enterprises such as the East India Company—ensured its early advantage in the race among European nations to obtain overseas territories, trade, and resources. At the beginning of the nineteenth century, Britain already held territories overseas, including parts of Canada, the Cape Colony in South Africa, Australia and New Zealand, and many West Indian islands.

After the defeat of Napoleon at Waterloo, and with a mighty navy that ruled the waves, Britain was able to expand its imperial holdings with renewed vigor. The East India Company expanded the British Empire in Asia, including the acquisition of Singapore in 1819 and parts of Burma in 1826 (acquired in its entirety in 1886 after the Anglo-Burmese Wars). In 1839 Britain secured Aden, and Hong Kong in 1841. After the Indian Mutiny of 1857, Britain took over the control of the vast subcontinent of India. New tropical colonies were acquired during "The Scramble for Africa" (see page 101), and in 1888 Britain installed protective troops on the strategically important Suez Canal (which was not owned or controlled by any one state).

VICTORIAN INNOVATORS: A CENTURY OF PROGRESS

The Victorian era was defined by the reign of British queen Victoria from 1837 until her death, in 1901. It was a long period of peace, prosperity, refined sensibilities, and a transition away from rationalism and toward romanticism and mysticism with regard to religion, social values, and the arts.

Charles Darwin (1809–1882): In 1831 Darwin joined a surveying expedition to South America aboard HMS *Beagle*. Over the course of the journey, he became a committed scientist and naturalist, and he published his theory of evolution by natural selection, *The Origin of Species*, in 1859.

(continued)

VICTORIAN INNOVATORS: A CENTURY OF PROGRESS *(continued)*

Thomas Edison (1847–1931): In 1878 and 1879 Joseph Swan in Britain and Thomas Edison in America both independently invented the electric lightbulb. Edison is credited with developing the first practical, long-lasting lightbulb.

Alexander Graham Bell (1847–1922): In 1876 the appropriately named Bell, a Scotsman living in the United States, invented the telephone by using telegraph technology to transmit the sound of voices. When it was demonstrated to Queen Victoria in 1878, she said it was "rather faint."

Henry Ford (1863–1947): An American industrialist, Ford is credited with the development of assembly-line production, which greatly influenced other manufacturing processes. His ability to produce inexpensive Ford motor cars triggered a revolution in transportation.

Other European Empires

In the nineteenth century the French Empire grew into the second-biggest colonial power after Britain. In 1830 the French began their conquest of Algeria; in 1881 France secured Tunisia as a protectorate; it acquired territories in Asia to form French Indochina in 1887. French enclaves were also secured in parts of China. By end of the 1800s the French had control of much of western, northern, and central Africa.

The Spanish empire effectively ended during the nineteenth century with the loss of all its American territories during the Napoleonic Wars and the Spanish-American Wars

THE IRISH QUESTION

Since the Act of Union in 1801, Ireland had been part of the United Kingdom, administered by the British government in Westminster. Much of the vast rural population of Ireland lived in abject poverty, made worse by the devastating blight that hit the Irish potato crop in 1845 and was followed by two bad harvests. The Great Famine struck, and by 1852 more than a million people had died. The famine strengthened feelings of mistrust toward Britain and increased calls for independence.

The Irish politician Charles Stewart Parnell ran a peaceful campaign for Home Rule (the reestablishment of an Irish Parliament responsible for internal affairs). By 1885 Parnell's Home Rule party had 86 members in Parliament and had convinced then prime minister William Gladstone that this was the solution to the "Irish Question." Gladstone twice tried to pass an Irish Home Rule Bill but was defeated by politicians who feared it might have a domino effect across the empire. Home Rule wasn't established for southern Ireland until the following century (see page 125).

of Independence. By the end of the century, Spain retained only its African territories in a small part of Morocco, Equatorial Guinea, and the western Sahara. Portugal similarly lost its South American settlements, later focusing on its bases in Africa, which included Angola and Mozambique. Late in the nineteenth century Bismarck's Germany claimed German South-West Africa, the Cameroons, and German East Africa. Belgium's Leopold II set himself up as sovereign of the Congo Free State in 1876.

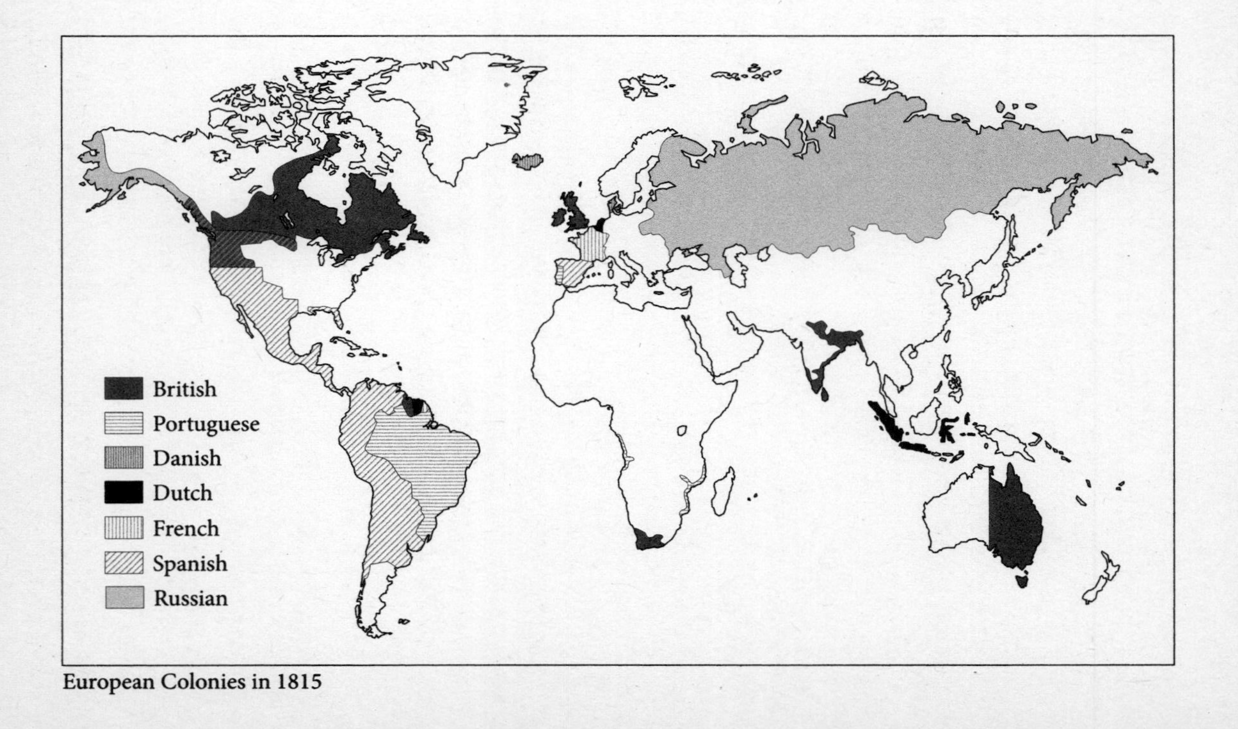

European Colonies in 1815

SETTLEMENT IN AUSTRALIA AND NEW ZEALAND

Captain James Cook sailed to the South Pacific in the late eighteenth century, mapping the coast of New Zealand in 1769 and landing in Botany Bay, Australia, in 1770. By 1788 Sydney Cove, Australia, was declared the first British penal settlement. Men (and some women) were transported for a range of crimes, mostly theft. With good conduct, they could be granted a ticket-of-leave—and be free to obtain paid work on the condition that they never left Australia. Voluntary immigration began in the 1820s, and squatter settlements, particularly in the east, led to violent conflict with the Aborigines. In 1901 Australia was declared a British Commonwealth state.

Settlers began arriving in New Zealand in the early nineteenth century, first setting up stations for seal and whale hunting and later establishing farms, mines, and permanent settlements. British sovereignty was declared in 1840, though fierce resistance from native Maori tribes continued. New Zealand became a self-governing dominion in 1907.

The Scramble for Africa

Since antiquity, North Africa has been colonized by a host of invaders, including the Greeks and Phoenicians, the Carthaginians, Romans, and Vandals. From the seventh century onward, Arabs, who brought Islamic culture and the Arabic language to North Africa and parts of East Africa, swept in. In the fifteenth century, Portugal and then other European nations explored much of the coastline of Africa, establishing outposts and implementing the African slave trade.

However, at the start of the nineteenth century, the vast interior of the continent was still largely untouched by Europeans until missionaries and explorers ventured farther in. French explorer René Caillié became the first European to survive a visit to Timbuktu in 1828. Scottish Protestant missionary David Livingstone explored the Zambezi River, discovering and renaming Victoria Falls in 1855. In 1866 he led an expedition in search of the source of the Nile, and his mysterious disappearance and death further sparked obsession with the African interior. John Hanning Speke and Sir Richard Burton became the first Europeans to reach Lake Tanganyika in 1858. Speke went on to reach another great lake, which he named Lake Victoria and which many consider to be the source of the Nile.

In the 1880s, armed with new information about Africa's untapped resources, particularly minerals and precious metals, European nations, led by Britain, France, and Germany, conducted a series of military campaigns against African nations in order to seize as much land as possible (called the "Scramble for Africa" after an 1884 conference in Berlin when European powers agreed upon the partition of the continent).

Wars raged across west, central, and eastern Africa as European colonial powers fought among themselves as well as with African nations. Key conflicts included the Anglo-Zulu War of 1879, the Sudan Campaign of 1885, and the Boer Wars (1880–1881 and 1899–1902). The Boers were Dutch settlers in South Africa. The Boer Wars ended in 1902 when the Boer Republics became British colonies, with the promise of self-government.

By the early twentieth century, most of Africa was under European control. Only Ethiopia and Liberia remained independent states.

- **French territory:** Parts of the west, north, and around the equator
- **German and Belgian territory:** Along the Congo
- **Portuguese territory:** Angola and Mozambique
- **British territory:** The east from South Africa to Egypt, as well as parts of the west (comprising 17 colonies and over 4 million square miles of land).

American Expansion

As the European empires expanded, the United States established itself farther into the North American continent, pushing westward toward the Pacific. Between 1850 and 1900, millions of Americans and European immigrants settled on the western plains and farther west beyond the Rocky Mountains.

In 1803 the United States effectively doubled its size when it purchased the Louisiana Territory from the French. By 1820 Florida, Missouri, and Maine had become part of the Union. By 1848—after conflicts with Mexico—Texas, California, and New Mexico had been included.

Meanwhile, the 1846 Oregon Treaty with Britain led to U.S. control of the Northwest, and a Mormon settlement was established in Salt Lake City, Utah. The 1848 gold rush in California brought an influx of settlers (the forty-niners) and created new towns, roads, and railroads, with other rushes following in the 1850s.

By the end of the Spanish-American War, in 1898, the United States had purchased Alaska from the Russians, annexed Hawaii, and taken control of Puerto Rico, Guam, and the Philippines, all of which secured the United States' status as a major world power.

The Slave Trade, the Abolition Movement, and the American Civil War

Since the 1500s, Europeans had been capturing Africans and transporting them as slaves to plantations on European colonies in the Americas, but the practice increased dramatically during the eighteenth century, until several hundred thousand Africans were being transported across the Atlantic each year. By 1800 half the population of Brazil was of African origin; by the mid-nineteenth century an estimated 9.5 million Africans had been transported to the New World.

The Africans were exchanged for export goods and forced to slave on European and then American plantations, where they lived a life of suffering and toil, working long hours, frequently abused and beaten. More than a million slaves also died on their way to the New World due to the appalling conditions in which they were kept.

In 1833 slavery was abolished in all British colonies. Thousands of slaves were freed by the British, and strict measures to enforce the laws against the slave trade were implemented. However, thousands of slaves were still being taken from West Africa and brought to America, Brazil, and Cuba, where demand for cotton and sugar was high.

In the United States, most of the industrialized northern states voluntarily abolished slavery by 1804. The cause of the abolitionists grew, and as many as 100,000 slaves are thought to have escaped to the North from the southern states via the Underground Railroad, a network of abolitionist sympathizers who protected and hid fugitive slaves on their way north. In 1852, **Harriet Beecher Stowe's** novel *Uncle Tom's Cabin* sold in the millions, and its stark depiction of the evils of slavery turned abolitionism into a moral crusade.

As America pursued its policy of westward expansion, tensions mounted between the industrialized states of the North, which had abandoned slavery, and the agricultural slave-owning states in the South. In 1854 the Republican Party was founded, largely in opposition to the extension of slavery. In 1860 **Abraham Lincoln,** a well-known opponent of slavery, became president. Fearing that Lincoln would attempt to extend the abolition of slavery across the United States, seven southern states split from the Union to form a Confederacy.

Hostilities started in 1861 when Confederate troops fired on Union forces at Fort Sumter in South Carolina. Four more states joined the rebel Confederates, and war was declared. At first the Confederates won victories led by such generals as "Stonewall" Jackson. But the Confederates' advance in the North was halted after the Battle of Gettysburg in 1863, while in the West the Union gained control of the Mississippi River at the Battle of Vicksburg. Union forces had more men and supplies and gradually the South was worn down as Union general William Tecumseh Sherman captured Atlanta, Georgia, and marched to the sea.

The Confederate leader **Robert E. Lee** eventually surrendered to the Union's lieutenant general **Ulysses S. Grant,** at Appomattox in April 1865. It was one of America's most brutal wars, with more than 600,000 soldiers and an undetermined number of civilians killed during hostilities.

After the American Civil War, Abraham Lincoln's **Emancipation Proclamation** of 1863 was finally put into practice, and slavery was abolished across all of the United States in 1865. In 1888 Brazil became the last South American country to abolish slavery. However, the legal practice of slavery in some countries, particularly in Africa and the Arab nations, continued into the twentieth century.

Colonial Wars

European empires were busy acquiring their dominions piecemeal, and as the century progressed, imperial nations were engaged in almost constant overseas conflict, as each empire struggled to expand and retain its territories in the face of either foreign aggression or internal mutiny. Key conflicts shaped the political boundaries of the globe and had far-reaching consequences for the great conflicts of the next century.

The Opium Wars (1839–1842 and 1856–1860)

In the early nineteenth century, British traders were intent on opening up trade in China to foreigners and were illegally exporting opium from India to China, to exchange for the latter's teas and silks. To prevent this and protect their opium trade, the Chinese seized and destroyed over twenty thousand chests of opium from British warehouses, whereupon the British sent a force of sixteen British warships to besiege Canton (Guangzhou) and advanced to Tianjin, threatening the capital Peking (Beijing) and capturing Shanghai in 1842. The war ended with the Treaty of Nanjing, in which Hong Kong was ceded to the British, and treaty ports were set up in China that would be open to British trade.

The Second Opium War broke out when the Qing dynasty authorities refused demands to renegotiate more favorable terms to the Nanjing treaty, and the French joined the British in launching a military attack on the Chinese. Beijing was overthrown, and the Chinese finally agreed to the Treaty of Tianjin in 1860, which provided freedom of travel to European, American, and Russian merchants and missionaries and opened ten more ports to Western trade.

The Indian Mutiny (1857–1858)

Since the 1600s, the East India Company had controlled a large part of India, building up an army made of British and local soldiers (the Bengal army). The Indian Mutiny began when sepoys (Indian soldiers under British command) in the Bengal army refused to use cartridges greased with pig and cow fat (offensive to Muslims and Hindus, respectively). The mutinies rapidly spread to Delhi and to most regiments of the Bengal army, as well as to a large section of the civilian population. In response, the British government transferred the control of India from the East India Company to the crown, managed by the India Office, a government department. Thereafter, a vast railroad network was built, and as trade prospered, India became a source of great wealth for Britain.

The Crimean War (1853–1856)

The Crimean War was one of the bloodiest wars in European history—as many as half of the 1.2 million soldiers who went out to fight lost their lives. It was fought by Russia against the allied forces of Turkey, Britain, France, and Piedmont and was caused by a long-running feud between the European powers over territories in the declining Ottoman Empire. War was triggered when Russian forces attacked a Turkish fleet. Britain and France, anxious to limit the ambitions of the Russians and protect trade routes, joined with Turkey to fight against the Russians.

Ill-equipped and badly prepared, thousands of allied troops succumbed to disease, though conditions improved with the intervention of **Florence Nightingale** ("The Lady with the Lamp") and her promotion of hygiene standards. The allied forces eventually won, and the Russians signed a peace treaty in 1856, but public opinion had already turned against the war because, for the first time, photographers such as Roger Fenton were able to show the realities of the conflict.

The Franco-Prussian War (1870–1871)

War between France and Prussia was provoked by the Prussian chancellor **Otto von Bismarck,** who predicted that a victorious war would lead to unification of Germany under Prussian leadership. Prussian forces, aided by a coalition of German states, advanced into France and defeated the French army at the Battle of Sedan, capturing the French emperor Napoleon III. German forces later laid siege to Paris, during which its population rose in revolt. In January 1871, the German states proclaimed their union under the new Prussian king, William I.

> **ECHOES OF THE PAST**
>
> Laws are like sausages—it is better not to see them being made.
>
> —Otto von Bismarck (1815–1898)

The war marked the end of the Second French Empire and the establishment of the Third French Republic. The German Empire swiftly became the dominant power in Continental Europe. Alsace and Lorraine were also ceded to Germany, a deep source of resentment for France and a contributing factor to World War I.

The Meiji Restoration and Japanese Imperialism

In 1853 and 1854 Commodore Matthew Perry of the U.S. Navy visited Japan (in the first steamship ever seen in Japan) and negotiated a treaty that opened two ports to U.S. trade. Treaties between Japan and other countries followed, but Japanese nationalists were unhappy with the treaty terms.

Armed opposition in 1868 eventually succeeded in replacing the shogunate with the Emperor Meiji Tennor (the Meiji Restoration). The Meiji Restoration ushered in a period of rapid industrialization, modernization, and military buildup. Feudalism was dismantled and Japan embarked on a series of military conflicts.

The First Sino-Japanese War (1894–1895) was the result of a rivalry between China and Japan over the control of Korea (a former vassal state of China). Chinese forces were rapidly overwhelmed by the superior Japanese forces, and the Chinese were forced to accept Korean independence and cede territories to Japan, including Taiwan.

The Russo-Japanese War (1904–1905) broke out between Japan and Russia over control of Korea and Manchuria. A surprise Japanese attack on Russian warships led to the destruction of Russian troops on both land and sea. This humiliating defeat led to the Russian Revolution of 1905, a shift of power balance in the East, and the type of warfare, with protracted battles and extended fronts, characteristic of World War I. Japan was now a world power.

Latin American Independence Movements

Strongly influenced by the American and French revolutions, revolutionary fervor swept through the Caribbean and Central and South America in the 1800s.

- **Haiti:** Pierre Toussaint L'Ouverture led a successful slave revolt against French plantation owners. Haiti became a free republic in 1804.

UNIFICATION OF ITALY AND GERMANY

One consequence of Napoleon's military campaigns was the intensifying of nationalistic feelings. As a result, Italy and Germany both managed to kick out foreign occupiers and become unified countries.

- **South America:** Bonaparte's installation of his brother, Joseph Bonaparte, on the Spanish throne incited revolution in the Spanish colonies of South America. In 1814 King Ferdinand VII was restored to the Spanish throne, but the colonies' quest for independence had already begun. Led by the brilliant general **Simón Bolívar,** the colonists declared independence for Venezuela in 1811. Independence was finally won in 1821. Meanwhile, another brilliant general, **José de San Martín,** had declared independence for Argentina in 1816, but the Spanish forces in Chile and Peru remained a threat. Bolívar and San Martín joined forces and defeated the Spanish in Peru in 1824, signaling the end of Spanish domination in South America.
- **Brazil.** After Napoleon's conquest of Portugal, Brazil was the home-in-exile for King John VI of Portugal. Eventually the king was able to return to Portugal, leaving his son Pedro in charge. Pedro declared Brazilian independence and named himself emperor. A revolt against the monarchy established Brazil as a republic in 1889.
- **Mexico.** A series of revolts against Spain resulted in independence in 1821 with the Treaty of Córdoba.

Chapter 8

World War I, Revolution, and Nationalism

After the Napoleonic Wars and the dissolution of the Holy Roman Empire, the Congress of Vienna, a conference of ambassadors from European nations was held from September 1814 to June 1815, to forge a peaceful balance of power in Europe. The result was the redrawing of the continent's political map, establishing the boundaries of France, the Duchy of Warsaw, the Netherlands, the states of the Rhine, the German province of Saxony, and various Italian territories. This created a balance of power in Europe, mainly among Britain, France, Austria, Prussia, and Russia. But by 1871, Britain and Prussia were clearly the most powerful in terms of economic and military strength.

Nationalism and military buildup in Europe led to the "war to end all wars," as one European nation after another was drawn into a large and industrialized war that caused unprecedented casualties. A punitive Treaty of Versailles ended the war and sowed the seeds of World War II by imposing unrealistically harsh conditions on Germany. The gap between the rich and poor, especially in Russia and China, became a major cause of revolution.

The Triple Entente and the Triple Alliance

By the start of the twentieth century, alliances between European powers were shifting. The Entente Cordiale, signed in 1904, formalized a "friendly agreement" between France and Britain, both of whom had become increasingly isolated in the latter half of the nineteenth century. The two countries had clashed over colonial interests in Morocco, Egypt, western Africa, and the Pacific. The Entente Cordiale settled overseas disputes and ensured that the two nations would not interfere in each other's empire-building.

A series of agreements with Russia, already an ally of France, then developed into the Triple Entente (which would form the basis of the Allied forces in World War I). The Entente was partly a response to the growing threat of Germany, which had been united under the Prussian "Iron Chancellor" Otto von Bismarck following the Franco-Prussian War (see page 109).

Germany had formed the Triple Alliance in 1882 with Italy and Austria-Hungary (later joined by the Ottoman Empire and Bulgaria) and had grown in military and industrial might in the later years of the nineteenth century. The new kaiser William II was intent on making Germany a world power. In 1898 he began an ambitious naval building program to challenge the maritime supremacy of Great Britain. Helmuth von Moltke, Germany's bellicose chief of general staff, sued for war—"the sooner the better." A fierce arms race between the two countries ensued, with the construction of powerful battleships. As the two nations fought for dominance on the sea and tensions mounted, other European powers looked to modernize their armed forces.

World War I

In Sarajevo on June 28, 1914, a young Bosnian Serb assassinated Archduke Franz Ferdinand, heir to the Austrian throne, for radical nationalist reasons. In retaliation, Austria-Hungary declared war on Serbia. One by one, through various entangling allegiances, all the other major European powers were drawn into the crisis.

Russia supported Serbia, assembling forces along its Austrian and German borders, causing Germany to declare war on Russia and its ally, France, in response. Germany, implementing its plan for a preemptive attack on France, invaded Belgium on August 3, 1914, resulting in Britain's declaring war on Germany on August 4, due to its obligation to protect Belgian neutrality.

The "war to end all wars" was one of the deadliest conflicts in history, with the mobilization of 70 million personnel and over 30 million military and civilian casualties (including 8.5 million war dead).

The Western Front

The Germans pushed back British forces in Belgium and crossed into northwest France, beginning an attack and counterattack between the Germans and the Allied forces as the two sides scrambled to the north in a race for the sea. By the end of the year, both sides had dug hundreds of miles of defensive trenches from the border of Switzerland to the

Belgian coast. Despite a series of major offensives, the line moved no more than 10 miles either way in the next three years. By the end of the war, 6,250 miles of trenches had been dug along the western front.

The key battles on the western front were fought at Ypres, Verdun, and the Somme. There were three major battles over the strategically situated city of Ypres between 1914 and 1917, with the third (known as the Battle of Passchendaele) resulting in over half a million casualties, with only a few miles of ground gained by the Allies. Despite a massive attack by the Germans on the French city of Verdun on February 21, 1916, the French forced them back. Later that year, the British and French forces tried to break through the German lines north of the river Somme leading to one of the bloodiest battles ever recorded, with more than 1.5 million casualties. Early mistakes cost the British dearly, and Allied forces only managed to advance six miles into German-held territory by the end of the battle in November 1916.

The Eastern Front and Other Theaters of War

On the eastern front, Russia unsuccessfully attempted to invade the German province of East Prussia in 1914, then had better luck holding the Austrian province of Galicia before being pushed back by Austro-Hungarian and German armies, losing Poland to the Germans in August 1915.

In the Middle East the Ottoman Empire's decision to ally itself with the Central Powers led to Britain sending an Anglo-Indian force to Mesopotamia (now part of Iraq) to protect its crucial oil supply. The Ottoman Turks attacked Suez in 1915 in an unsuccessful retaliation. After failed Allied naval attacks on the strategically important Ottoman-controlled Dardanelles Strait (in order to threaten the Turkish capital of Constantinople), British, French, Australian, and New Zealand troops invaded Turkey from the sea twice in 1915, landing on the Gallipoli Peninsula. However, they were forced to retreat in 1916. As a result of these defeats, the Allies redoubled their presence in the Middle East, finally breaking through the Ottoman lines at Gaza in October 1917. A force of British, New Zealand, and Australian troops occupied Jerusalem in December, followed by Damascus and Aleppo. Meanwhile, the Mesopotamian campaign culminated in the capture of Baghdad in March 1917. By the end of October 1918, the Ottoman Empire had signed an armistice.

In Africa, meanwhile, with 3 million Commonwealth soldiers coming to Britain's aid in the war, it is unsurprising that they and France attempted to expand their empires by using forces from their territories to target German colonies in western Africa, capturing Togoland in 1914 and Kamerun (now Cameroon) in 1916. German South-West Africa fell in 1915. However, a vast force of British, African, and Indian troops had been tied up in German East Africa by a small force of Germans and Africans, which only surrendered two weeks after the armistice had been signed.

The Italians joined the Allies in 1915, though due to poor preparation suffered huge casualties in disastrous attacks on Italy's mountainous borders with Austria and were finally scattered before a combined Austro-Hungarian and German attack at Caporetto in late 1917. The remaining Italian force, strengthened by Allied reinforcements after their retreat, took revenge at the Battles of the Piave River and Vittorio Veneto, taking half a million Austrian prisoners and restoring the prewar border.

WOMEN'S SUFFRAGE

As early as 1694, Mary Astell wrote, "If all men are born free, how is it that all women are born slaves?" Mary Wollstonecraft picked up the feminist theme with *A Vindication of the Rights of Women* in 1792. The first countries to extend limited voting rights to women were Sweden, Britain, and some western states in the United States in the 1860s. In 1893 the British colony of New Zealand became the first self-governing nation to extend the right to vote to all adult (white) women, and the women of the colony of South Australia achieved the same right in 1895. The first European country to introduce women's suffrage was the Grand Principality of Finland, which was then a part of the Russian Empire with autonomous powers. The United States didn't follow until 1920. The last European country to grant equal voting rights to women was Switzerland in 1971.

At sea, despite massive prewar naval building, the only major battle, fought in 1916 near Jutland (Denmark), was inconclusive. However, Germany's concentration on submarine warfare, with its fleet of U-boats targeting Allied merchant and troop ships, caused many problems for the Allies, and was a contributing factor—particularly after the sinking of the *Lusitania*, a passenger ship, in 1915—to the United States' crucial decision to join the war in 1917.

The End of World War I

In spring 1918 the Germans launched a massive campaign on the western front using troops transferred from the eastern front following a treaty with Russia (see page 116). However, with the help of the Americans, the Allied line held. By the time the Allies counterattacked and pierced the previously impregnable Hindenburg Line, the worn-out German army was forced to retreat. On November 7, 1918, Germany surrendered, and on November 11, the armistice was signed.

Versailles and Other Treaties

The **Treaty of Versailles** concluded peace terms between the Allied forces and Germany and was one of the main postwar settlements of 1919–1923. The talks were dominated by the United States, Britain, and France. Germany was made to accept sole responsibility for the war and to pay reparations to the Allies for damage caused in the war. Germany's armed forces were to be strictly limited. All German colonial possessions were given up, along with territories in Europe, including ceding Alsace-Lorraine to France and west Prussia to the restored nation of Poland. The **League of Nations** was set up as a peacekeeping organization, and Germany was not allowed to become a member until it had shown itself to be a peaceful country, which it did in 1926.

Other treaties were signed at the Paris Peace Conference with Bulgaria, Austria-Hungary, and Turkey. Bulgaria was forced to pay reparations, accept limits to its army, and cede territory to Romania, Greece, and Yugoslavia. The Habsburg empire of Austria-Hungary was effectively dismantled, as

THE DECLINE OF THE OTTOMAN EMPIRE

By the early twentieth century, the Ottoman Empire was in terminal decline due in part to the expansion of western European empires and the discovery of new trade routes. By the end of the Balkan Wars in 1913, the Ottomans had lost most of their European and North African territories. They lost more provinces in Arabia and Greece during World War I. In 1922, the caliphate was abolished and the Republic of Turkey declared. In Persia, Reza Shah Pahlavi deposed the ruling shah in 1925 and set about modernizing the country, changing the name of the nation to Iran.

Poland and the newly created Czechoslovakia became independent states, and all occupied territories were surrendered and its navy dismantled.

The Ottoman Empire was divided up under the Treaty of Sèvres and then again, after a war with Greece, at Lausanne in 1923. Turkey retained some of its Greek territory, but ceded Syria under a French League of Nations mandate and Iraq, Palestine, and Jordan under a British mandate. Other territories were given up to Greece and Italy, and the Dardanelles was overseen by the League of Nations.

The Russian Revolutions

When it entered World War I, Russia was already experiencing a great deal of social unrest. Heavy taxation had brought mounting distress to the poor, and Russia's involvement and eventual defeat in its war with Japan (see page 110) aggravated discontent.

The Revolution of 1905

On January 9, 1905, later called "Bloody Sunday," peaceful demonstrators demanding higher wages and shorter hours were fired on by government troops in St. Petersburg; 150 people were killed and the czar was further discredited. The result was the Revolution of 1905, with strikes across the country and mutinies within the armed forces. Nicholas II was forced to grant a constitution providing for a duma (parliament). However, disorder and strikes continued as Russia entered World War I, struggling to supply its troops at the front and suffering huge casualties (more than 5 million men by 1917).

The February Revolution

In February 1917, after a winter of poverty and hunger, there were renewed disturbances in St. Petersburg (renamed Petrograd) in which the troops ordered to fire on striking protesters refused and instead joined the uprising. The uprising culminated with the czar's abdication and the formation of the Russian Provisional Government.

CZAR NICHOLAS II (1868–1918)

Overshadowed by his more charismatic and forceful father, Alexander III, Nicholas II was a weak and wavering czar, subject to the will of the advisers around him. In spite of his weakness, or because of it, the last of the Romanov czars clung to the idea of his supreme right to rule—and was out of touch with the mood of the people. Nicholas was forced to abdicate in 1917 following the February Revolution (see above), and he and his family were finally shot by the Bolsheviks in 1918.

The October Revolution and Civil War

In the October Revolution of 1917, **Vladimir Lenin's** Bolshevik Party seized power. The **Bolsheviks** took over the government entirely, promising "peace, bread, and land" to the Russian people. The Germans had offered the first of these, but with the punitive terms of the Treaty of Brest-Litovsk, which the Bolsheviks signed in March 1918. It was one of the most brutal treaties in history, forcing Russia to cede 60 million people, almost a third of its agricultural land, and more than three-quarters of its coal reserves. Civil war ensued between the Reds (the Bolsheviks) and the Whites (the more conservative anti-Bolshevik Russians). The Russian Communist Party, as the Bolsheviks called themselves from 1918, gained supremacy and established the **Soviet Union** in 1922.

During the civil war Lenin oversaw practices of state terror in the form of torture and summary execution of anyone opposed to the revolution. All industry was placed under state control and any nonconformity with Bolshevism was treated as counterrevolutionary. In 1918 Lenin was shot twice. He seemingly recovered but suffered subsequent strokes. The civil war was over by 1920, but the economy was in a state of collapse. Lenin allowed small-scale industries to be denationalized but retained a viselike grip on political dissent.

Joseph Vissarionovich Dzhugashvili joined the Bolsheviks under Lenin and in 1913 adopted the name **Stalin** (man of steel). He became the Communist Party's general secretary. Following Lenin's death in 1924, Stalin sidelined **Leon Trotsky,** who had helped Lenin organize the October Revolution, to become the uncontested leader by 1927. In the following year he launched programs to expand and collectivize farming and rapidly develop industry. Millions of

KEY TERMS OF COMMUNISM

Marxism: The economic theory derived from the doctrines of **Friedrich Engels** and **Karl Marx,** which states that the economy is at the root of all social oppression. In Marx's model, capitalism is doomed to failure because revolution of the proletariat is inevitable.

Communism: A political system in which there is shared ownership of property and whose ideal is of a classless society, as laid out in Marx and Engels's *Communist Manifesto* of 1848.

Socialism: Economic theory favoring cooperation as opposed to capitalist competition. Early socialists didn't believe in armed revolution, and their view of politics was directly challenged by Marx. Lenin defined socialism as the transitional stage between capitalism and Communism.

---

peasants who resisted were shot or sent to labor camps, while others died from famine as the government seized grain from producers. Stalin eliminated political opposition in the Great Purges of 1936–1938 as the intelligentsia, members of the party, army officers, and millions of others were executed or sent to labor camps in Siberia.

Civil War in China

The **Boxer Rebellion** of 1900 was a rebellion of Chinese workers and poor peasants who resented the privileges granted to foreigners. The Boxers, or Society of Righteous and Harmonious Fists, used the slogan "Death to the foreign devils." Though the Qing dynasty expressed sympathy for the

rebellion, it did not back it up with military might. A multinational force drawn from Britain, France, Germany, Austria, Italy, Russia, Japan, and the United States descended upon China and quickly squelched the rebellion. Despite the defeat of the rebellion, or perhaps because of it, the discontent of the Chinese people with foreign intervention was the beginning of the end of imperial rule in China.

The Republic of China

In 1912 The Nationalist Party, or **Kuomintang,** under **Sun Yat-sen** succeeded in overthrowing the Qing dynasty, which had ruled since 1644. Sun Yat-sen had hoped to establish a strong democracy, based on Western ideals, though without the intervention of foreign countries. He was not able to unify the entire country, and much power remained in the hands of provincial warlords. Meanwhile, Europe was engaged in World War I. The weak government in Beijing declared war against Germany to align itself with the Allied forces. Then came the Treaty of Versailles, which took former Chinese territories that had been controlled by Germany and gave them to Japan. Thus rebuffed by the West, Sun Yat-sen turned to the Soviet Union, aligning the Kuomintang with the Chinese Communist Party, which was founded in 1920 by **Mao Zedong** and others.

After Sun Yat-sen's death in 1925, **Chiang Kai-shek** took over as the head of the Kuomintang. A strong leader, Chiang Kai-shek was able to wrest control from the provincial warlords and attempted to eliminate the Communist Party. In 1928 Chiang Kai-shek became president of the **Nationalist Republic of China,** and the United States and Great Britain formally recognized the new government.

Chiang Kai-shek's suppression of the Communist Party led to civil war, which raged from 1930 to 1937. This conflict ended with the invasion of the Japanese in 1937. But 1938, Japan controlled much of China, and the Nationalists and Communists maintained an uneasy peace until the end of World War II.

Indian Nationalism

Since the mid-1800s Indian nationalism had been growing, fostered by upper-class Indians who attended British schools. Two groups formed to promote Indian independence: the Indian National Congress and the Muslim League, which demanded a separate homeland. Then came World War I, and more than a million Indians enlisted in the British army. In return for their service, the British government promised

ECHOES OF THE PAST

An eye for an eye only ends up making the whole world blind.

—Mohandas K. Gandhi (1869–1948)

reforms that did not materialize. The massacre of nationalist demonstrators by British troops at Amritsar in 1919 further intensified anti-British sentiment.

Mohandas K. Gandhi emerged as a leader of the independence movement, preaching civil disobedience, even in the face of brutal oppression. Eventually, Great Britain granted limited self-rule in 1935. Competing visions of India's future, however, only served to increase tension between Hindus (the majority population) and Muslims.

The Anglo-Irish Conflict

The issue of Home Rule in Ireland had long been fiercely debated in government. In 1914 Prime Minister Asquith finally passed the Home Rule Act, which reinstated a limited form of self-government in Ireland, but crucially held back application of this law until after World War I. However, many Protestants in the northeast of Ireland were opposed to majority rule by Irish Catholics in the south. Unionists in Ulster formed the Ulster Volunteers and prepared to seize power as soon as the act came into effect: Ireland was on the brink of civil war.

The 1916 Easter Rising

Radical republican groups, led by the Irish Republican Brotherhood (IRB) and supported by the Irish National Volunteers, saw Britain's preoccupation with the war as the perfect time to stage an uprising. On Easter Monday, 1916, rebels seized the General Post Office in Dublin and proclaimed an Irish republic. After six days of fighting, the rebellion was crushed, 16 of its leaders executed, and more than two thousand men and women imprisoned. While the uprising itself failed, the reprisals served to radicalize opinion, turning many moderates against the British and laying the foundations for the Irish War of Independence.

The Establishment of the Irish Free State

Following Britain's heavy handling of the Easter Rising, Irish voters overwhelmingly supported the separatist political party **Sinn Fein** in elections two years later. Sinn Fein's military arm, the **IRA (Irish Republican Army)** under **Michael Collins,** mounted a savage guerrilla war against the British army and paramilitary forces (the Black and Tans and the Auxiliaries). The campaign was called the Irish War of Independence (1919–1921), and atrocities were committed by both sides.

In December 1921 Prime Minister **David Lloyd George** negotiated the Anglo-Irish Treaty, which gave separate dominion status to Ireland as an Irish Free State, with the exception of six counties in Ulster that formed Northern Ireland. Hard-line nationalists, who believed that all of Ireland should be a republic, remained opposed to the treaty. A two-year civil war (1922–1923) between rival republican factions spread throughout the country and led to the death of Michael Collins. Thereafter, aspects of the treaty were gradually dismantled until the south declared itself a republic in all but name in the constitution of 1937. In 1948 this declaration was made official, with Britain formally acknowledging the **Republic of Eire** in 1949.

You are joking, aren't you?

Chapter 9

World War II

The Great Depression of the 1930s started in the United States and quickly traveled worldwide, bringing with it widespread unemployment and economic hardship. People turned to authoritarian leaders for relief. Fascism arose in Italy and Germany. Italy, Germany, and Japan began aggressive campaigns to seize new territories, setting the stage for World War II.

World War II started on September 1, 1939, and ended on September 2, 1945. The war covered territories of Europe, the Pacific, the Atlantic, Southeast Asia, China, the Middle East, the Mediterranean, and Africa. All in all, about 62 million people died during and leading up to the conflict. At the end of World War II, the global map was redrawn once again.

The Rise of Italian Fascism

Benito Mussolini (who had been an elementary school teacher before becoming the dictator of Italy) founded a Fascist force in 1919. Mussolini had been a radical socialist, but he turned away from it, embracing the antisocialist, anticapitalist ideals of Fascism. Mussolini became prime minister in 1922 and assumed the title Il Duce (the leader).

Mussolini's nationalist ideas spread across Europe, inspiring Hitler's vision of the German Reich and informing the nationalist political ideals of General Franco during the Spanish Civil War (see below). Unlike Hitler, Mussolini was hindered by a dominant elite and a monarch. Though he pursued an aggressive foreign policy during the Abyssinia Crisis (opposite) and as a German ally in World War II, both wars proved unpopular. He was deposed in 1943. Italy signed an armistice with the Allies in the same year and joined in the fight against Germany. Mussolini fled into exile and was shot by Italian partisans in 1945.

The Spanish Civil War

The Spanish Civil War began in 1936 with a military coup against the socialist Republican government of Spain. It was led by a group of right-wing army generals, fearful of the reforms that the government was planning. The country was divided, with the Nationalist rebels gaining control of much of the north. The armed forces were also split, but most of the army, navy, and air force remained loyal to the Republicans.

THE ABYSSINIA CRISIS (1935)

The Abyssinia Crisis was a diplomatic crisis resulting from Italy's invasion of Abyssinia (now Ethiopia) in 1935. The weakness of the League of Nations was exposed when it was unable either to control Italy or to protect Ethiopia, both member states. The war resulted in the military occupation of Ethiopia, the exile of its emperor **Haile Selassie,** and the annexation of Ethiopia into the newly created colony of Italian East Africa. It wasn't until World War II that British troops evicted the Italians from Ethiopia (as well as from Eritrea and Somalia).

It was the Nationalist's intervention of Nazi Germany and Fascist Italy that swayed the balance. The Republican government was aided by the Soviet Union as well as thousands of individual volunteers from Europe and the United States. Picasso's painting *Guernica* famously depicts the bombing of the town of the same name by Nationalist forces in 1937, but both sides were guilty of brutality. By December 1938 the Nationalists defeated the Republican armies, and on March 5 the Republican government was forced into exile. The war ended in April 1939 with the victory of the Nationalists and the founding of a Fascist dictatorship under General Franco.

A Global Depression Sets the Stage for WWII

The economy of the United States in the 1920s seemed prosperous, but it was seriously flawed, with an uneven distribution of wealth and an overproduction of manufactured goods and food.

At the time, American factories were producing about half of the world's industrial goods. But as a result of overproduction, factories began laying off workers. As more workers lost their jobs, families bought fewer goods. As more efficient farming methods produced a surplus of American-grown food at the same time as competition began from abroad, farmers began defaulting on their mortgages. Unpaid debts weakened banks and forced some to close. Still, financial markets appeared strong, and middle-income people bought stocks by paying a small percentage of the stock's price as a down payment and borrowing the rest from a stockbroker.

In September of 1929, some investors began to feel that stock prices were too high. Anticipating a drop in prices, they began to sell. The sell-off continued until October 29, 1929, when the stock market crashed. By 1932 unemployment was nearly 25 percent; thousands of businesses failed and banks closed.

The collapse of the U.S. economy sent shock waves around the world. American investors withdrew money from Europe and trade dropped sharply.

Hitler and Nazi Germany

Austrian-born Adolf Hitler had fought and been wounded in World War I and was profoundly affected by Germany's defeat and the humiliating terms of the Treaty of Versailles. One of many disaffected agitators against Germany's postwar government, he swiftly became leader of a small nationalist party, which became the National Socialist German Workers' Party, or Nazi Party, in 1922. After the Munich "beer-hall putsch" of 1923, when he and others attempted to seize power in Bavaria, Hitler was imprisoned. He used this time to compose his political manifesto *Mein Kampf* (My Struggle).

Hitler used *Mein Kampf* to outline his political goals. He argued that the German "race" was superior to all other races, and that Jews and Communists were the main threats to Germany. He believed that a Jewish conspiracy existed that was attempting world domination and that it was up to the Germans to save humanity.

The **Great Depression,** which followed the **Wall Street Crash of 1929,** resulted in 6 million Germans being unemployed. The nationalist Nazi Party, led by Hitler, promised to restore national pride and create jobs. Taking a popular stance, he railed against the Treaty of Versailles, which had crippled the country. The Nazi Party steadily gained electoral strength over the next several years.

In 1933 Hitler became chancellor and swiftly established a one-party dictatorship, eliminating his rivals in the "Night of the Long Knives," a series of political murders. Following President Paul von Hindenburg's death a year later, Hitler appointed himself president and *Führer* (leader) of the German Reich (state), and thereafter assumed total control of the country.

With his authority at home unchallenged, Hitler began rearming Germany, in violation of the Treaty of Versailles, reoccupying the Rhineland in 1936, annexing Austria in 1938, and beginning the piecemeal occupation of Czechoslovakia. Desperate to avoid war, Britain and France adopted a policy of **appeasement** toward Hitler, with Prime Minister **Neville Chamberlain** declaring "peace in our time" following his return from the Munich Conference in 1938. But as German tanks advanced into the rest of Czechoslovakia, Britain abandoned its policy of appeasement and promised to defend Poland should Hitler invade it.

World War II

In the early hours of September 1, 1939, Germany launched the **blitzkrieg** (lightning war), a combined attack of fast-moving tanks, troops, and dive-bombers. Tanks rolled into

Poland from the west, while Soviet forces invaded from the east, the result of a secret Nazi-Soviet pact agreed in August. Soon after, Britain and France declared war on Germany. For a few months, there followed a "phony war," in which little happened as Hitler regrouped his forces. This came to an end in April 1940, when Germany invaded Denmark and then Norway, followed by Holland and Belgium. As these countries fell, Hitler advanced into France, leading to the Allies suffering one of the worst military disasters of the war.

The War on Land

By May 24, 1940, thousands of Allied troops were trapped on the beaches around Dunkirk, having been cut off by a German advance in northern France. Prime Minister **Winston Churchill,** who had recently succeeded the ineffectual Chamberlain, ordered an emergency evacuation. In nine days, the Royal Navy, aided by hundreds of civilian craft, carried some 338,000 British and French troops back to the United Kingdom. Three weeks after the evacuation of Dunkirk, France surrendered to the Germans.

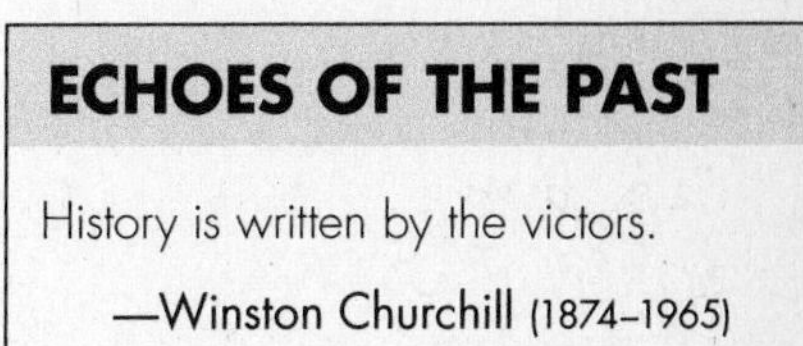

General **Charles de Gaulle** escaped to Britain and established the Free French Forces and a French government-in-exile. The Nazis occupied the north and west of France, while a pro-German puppet government was installed under Marshal Pétain at Vichy, in the so-called free zone. From 1942, following the Allied invasions of Vichy French territories in North Africa, German forces occupied all of France,

THE HOLOCAUST

Nazi ideology centered on a belief in the superiority of the German race and held that Germany could achieve domination only by purging the nation of "weak groups," which included Jews, Gypsies, Communists, homosexuals, and the mentally disabled. Hitler targeted Jews in particular, and on coming to power in 1933, he began to exclude them from German society. The Nuremberg Laws of 1935 deprived Jews of citizenship; by 1937 Jewish businesses were being confiscated and anti-Semitic propaganda circulated.

In the *Kristallnacht* (Crystal Night, from the broken glass that lay on the streets) of November 9, 1938, synagogues were burned down and Jewish shops looted. Many Jews fled Germany and Austria and moved abroad (often forced to leave their property and assets to be seized by the Nazis). As the Nazis occupied other European countries the persecutions spread, with forced-labor concentration camps and mass shootings.

The extermination camps were built to provide the "final solution" to the Jewish "problem." Six extermination camps equipped with gas chambers were built in Poland. Jews were transported to these camps from all over Nazi-occupied Europe; nearly 6 million Jews were killed, along with Soviet, Polish, and other POWs, political and religious opponents, captured enemy agents, people with disabilities, and other minority groups.

---

enforcing Nazi laws, with Vichy collaboration, and deporting French Jews and resistance workers to Germany, where most died in the camps.

In June 1941 Hitler advanced into Russia, toward the oilfields of the Caucasus. After huge territorial gains, the main German advance was barred by the Soviet defense of

SECOND SINO-JAPANESE WAR (1937–1945)

War broke out once more in the Far East as China attempted to seize back territory that the Japanese had begun occupying from 1931. Stalemate ensued and Japanese forces were diverted to World War II; Japan's eventual defeat by the Americans resulted in the restoration of Chinese territories to China.

Stalingrad in southwestern Russia. The Germans reached the center, but the massive Soviet counterattack trapped them in the city. The German commander in chief surrendered in January 1943. With as many as 2 million military and civilian casualties on both sides, the disastrous German defeat halted Germany's advance into Russia and marked a major turning point in the war.

Another turning point for the Allies occurred in late 1942 at El Alamein on the Egyptian coast. General Bernard Montgomery's British forces (aided by troops from South Africa, New Zealand, and Australia, as well as Free French and Greek forces) secured a decisive victory and prevented German field marshal Erwin Rommel's forces from occupying Egypt and advancing toward the Suez Canal.

The War at Sea

The Battle of the Atlantic was a struggle kept up throughout the war between German and Allied forces for domination of the shipping routes to Britain. German U-boats (submarines) were the main weapon of attack; they claimed an average of 96 ships per month in 1942. However, by 1943 better radar and intelligence gleaned through the British decryption of the German cipher machine, Enigma, enabled Britain to reroute

THE ATLANTIC CHARTER

Early on in the war, President Franklin Roosevelt and Prime Minister Winston Churchill met and agreed on the Allied goals for the postwar world. The Atlantic Charter was a pivotal policy statement that was later agreed to by all the Allies.

The charter stated the ideal goals of the war: no territorial aggrandizement; no territorial changes made against the wishes of the people; restoration of self-government to those deprived of it; free access to raw materials; reduction of trade restrictions; global cooperation to secure better economic and social conditions for all; freedom from fear and want; freedom of the seas; and abandonment of the use of force, as well as disarmament of aggressor nations.

This document was critical in shaping the world after the war, particularly in terms of Africa.

---

convoys away from U-boat "wolf packs." Enigma intelligence was also crucial to Allied victories in North Africa, Italy, and Normandy.

Meanwhile, the Japanese had set their sights upon unprotected British, French, and Dutch colonial possessions in Asia and the Pacific. On December 7, 1941, they attacked the U.S. Pacific Fleet's base at Pearl Harbor, Hawaii, sinking several ships, and thereby provoking the United States to join the war on the side of the Allies. (Churchill said he slept "the sleep of the saved" that night.)

Aided by decrypted communication, the U.S. fleet ambushed and defeated the Japanese fleet at the Battle of the Coral Sea in May 1942 and the Battle of Midway the following month. Thereafter, the U.S. Navy, with British, Australian, and

> **ECHOES OF THE PAST**
>
> Experience has shown how deeply the seeds of war are planted by economic rivalry and social injustice.
>
> —Harry S. Truman (1884–1972)

other forces in support, ultimately succeeded in defeating Japanese naval power in the Pacific, leading to the eventual recapture of several Japanese-occupied territories through a series of amphibious operations, including the assaults on Iwo Jima, Guadalcanal, and Okinawa.

The War in the Air

After the fall of France, Hitler launched a bombing offensive against Britain as a prelude to invasion, attacking shipping and ports, then airfield and communication centers in southern England. However, the Germans met significant resistance from the Royal Air Force during the Battle of Britain (August–October 1940) and suffered heavy losses from fighter aircraft and ground defenses, crucially assisted by radar, then highly secret. On October 12 Hitler postponed and ultimately abandoned his invasion of Britain, codenamed Operation Sea Lion.

Nevertheless, between September 1940 and May 1941, the sustained bombing of British cities, known as the **Blitz,** continued, with the intended goal of demoralizing Britain into surrender. Over the course of the Blitz, 2 million buildings were seriously damaged or destroyed and sixty thousand civilians killed.

The sustained American and British strategic bombing of Germany proved even more devastating. Between May 1942 and July 1945 German factories and military zones

THE ATOMIC BOMB

Between 1934 and 1939, much work was being done in the scientific community to understand the nature of the atom. In 1938 scientists in Germany succeeded in splitting the atom. Concerned that Nazi Germany was developing an atomic bomb, **Dr. Leo Szilard,** a Hungarian refugee who had fled from Nazi persecution, wrote to President Roosevelt urging him to start an American effort to develop its own nuclear weapon. **Albert Einstein,** whose theory of relativity provided the theoretical framework for splitting the atom, cosigned the letter.

As a result, the U.S. government undertook what was known as the **Manhattan Project,** with the goal of being the first to produce an atomic bomb. Scientist **Robert Oppenheimer** led the project.

The first test of the atomic bomb took place in the desert near Los Alamos, New Mexico, on July 16, 1945. The huge explosion created a characteristic mushroom cloud of radioactive vapor, and all that remained of the soil at the blast site were fragments of jade-green radioactive glass created by the heat of the reaction. The brilliant light from the detonation was seen more than 120 miles away. Upon witnessing the explosion, its creators had mixed reactions. Several participants signed petitions against using the bomb, but their protests were ignored.

A uranium bomb nicknamed "Little Boy" was dropped on Hiroshima on August 6, 1945. The bomb instantly killed 66,000 people and injured 69,000 others. The bomb blast vaporized an area about half a mile in diameter. There was total destruction within one mile of the bomb site, and severe blast damage was sustained for an area of two miles in diameter. Within a diameter of two and a half miles, everything flammable burned. The remaining area of the blast zone was riddled with serious blazes that stretched out to the final edge, a little over three miles in diameter.

On August 9, 1945, a plutonium bomb nicknamed "Fat Man" was dropped on Nagasaki. It leveled nearly half the city, killed thirty-nine thousand people, and injured more than twenty-five thousand people. Japan offered to surrender on August 10, 1945. Over time more people would die from radiation poisoning and still more from leukemia and other cancers caused by radioactive fallout from both bombs.

The use of atomic weapons was a game-changer for both World War II and the postwar era. The buildup of atomic weapons by both the United States and the Soviet Union resulted in the Cold War. Today as many as eight nations acknowledge the possession of nuclear weapons. This nuclear club includes the United States,

(continued)

THE ATOMIC BOMB *(continued)*

the United Kingdom, Russia, France, the People's Republic of China, India, Pakistan, and North Korea.

The nuclear weapons of today are far more deadly than the bombs dropped on Japan. Also, with the development of intercontinental ballistic missiles, the delivery of atomic bombs has become easier. In 1966, during the Cold War, as many as 32,193 nuclear warheads and bombs were built and ready for deployment. Many more developing countries are in the process of acquiring the technology to build nuclear weapons. International efforts are under way to undertake large-scale voluntary nuclear disarmament. Still, one of the greatest fears is that a terrorist group will mix radioactive material with a conventional weapon to create a so-called dirty bomb.

---

were targeted, as well as towns and cities, notably Hamburg, Dresden, and Berlin. An estimated 750,000 to 1 million German civilians were killed in total.

D-Day Landings and Victory in Europe

By 1944 the German hold on Europe was weakening and the Allied invasion of Normandy was begun with the aim of liberating Western Europe and taking the pressure off Soviet forces fighting on the eastern front. On June 6, 1944, the Germans were caught off-guard as 156,000 men landed on five Normandy beaches. Allied forces eventually broke through the German defenses; by August 25, the Allies had liberated Paris.

Thereafter, the Allies pushed through Europe, despite heavy casualties during the Battle of the Bulge in the Ardennes and at Arnhem in Holland. In March 1945, they crossed the Rhine and entered Germany, linking up with the advancing Soviet army in April. Realizing he was defeated, Hitler shot himself on April 30. On May 8, 1945, the Allies accepted Germany's unconditional surrender and declared victory in Europe.

The End of the War

In July and August 1945, following the German surrender, the leaders of the "big three" Allied nations of the Soviet Union, the United States, and Britain met at the Potsdam Conference. Stalin, President Harry S. Truman (who succeeded President Franklin D. Roosevelt), and Churchill (later replaced by Clement Attlee) agreed on the terms of Germany's reparations and its division into four Allied occupation zones.

Meanwhile, British and Commonwealth forces defeated the Japanese in India and Burma. The American amphibious assaults on Japanese-controlled territory were successful, but Japan refused to surrender. The United States proceeded with dropping atomic bombs on Hiroshima and Nagasaki on August 6 and 9, 1945. About 140,000 Japanese civilians died immediately, and many more later perished or suffered from radiation poisoning. On September 2, 1945, the Japanese surrendered and World War II was over. More than 50 million lives had been lost during the war.

Chapter 10

The New Globalism

Two world wars dissolved the colonial empires that had formed over the last two centuries. They devastated nations, left 60 million dead and 50 million people displaced, and caused property damage that ran into the billions of dollars. Agriculture was disrupted, and hunger was a constant in postwar Europe. Japan was in ruins, occupied by the U.S. army. A new constitution changed Japan into a constitutional monarchy.

The United Nations was formed in 1945 to ensure peace and stability, but hostility prevailed between Western nations and the Soviet Union as the superpowers struggled for supremacy in the Cold War. Former colonies become new nations and countries struggled for democracy. Mass communications, rapid transportation, the Internet, and global trade continue to transform our world.

The United Nations

The United Nations (UN) was set up in 1945 as a successor to the failed League of Nations, with the aim of ensuring peace, security, and cooperation among the nations of the world. In 1942, 26 Allied nations signed the Declaration of the United Nations and pledged to continue fighting together against Nazi Germany and the Axis powers. President Franklin Roosevelt decided America should take the lead, and for this reason, the first U.N. Conference on International Organization took place in San Francisco on April 25, 1945. In June 1946, 50 member nations signed the Charter of the United Nations and headquarters were set up in New York. The United Nations grew rapidly as former colonial territories gained independence and applied for membership. As of this writing, the United Nations has 193 member nations.

The Creation of Israel

In 1947 U.N. leaders voted that Palestine should be divided up into a Jewish state and an Arab state, with Jerusalem under U.N. governance. Palestine had been under a British mandate since the end of World War I, and Britain formally established the Zionist Jewish Agency to represent Jewish interests in the region in 1929. However, the Arab states rejected partition, and the newly formed Zionist government declared an independent state of Israel. Arab-Israeli wars over territories continued over the following decades, as Israel enlarged its territories, and conflict in the region continues to the present day.

The Partition of India (1947)

India was granted independence from Britain in 1947 and divided into two states: India and the Muslim state of Pakistan. Partition marked the end of the British Empire, but it also displaced millions of people, and led to the deaths of hundreds of thousands in the ensuing unrest between Hindus and Muslims.

Unscrambling Africa

After World War II the United States and the African colonies put pressure on Britain to abide by the terms of the Atlantic Charter, which called for self-government for all nations that want it.

At the same time, there was a strong nationalist movement in Africa, led by returning soldiers. Because they had fought to protect the interests of the colonial powers, the veterans expected reward, only to return to the exploitation and indignities of colonial rule. Discontent with colonial rule increased.

In 1945 the Pan-African Congress in Manchester, England, marked a turning point because it attempted to address the needs of all blacks. Pan-Africanism stressed the common experiences of blackness and sought the liberation of all black people around the world. African leaders became more influential in the movement, and they used it to attack colonial rule. The movement became more African-based after 1945.

One of the legacies of the colonial period in Africa was the creation of national borders that showed little regard for ethnic groups. Some borders separated linked ethnic groups; others enclosed traditional enemies. Pan-Africanism proved

END OF APARTHEID IN SOUTH AFRICA

South Africa became an independent member of the British Commonwealth in 1931. The white minority government imposed a harsh policy of strict racial segregation known as apartheid in 1948. Blacks were required to live in "homelands," and economic and educational opportunities were severely limited. Unrest and violent government reprisals led to international condemnation and trade restrictions. Apartheid officially ended in 1996 with the adoption of a new constitution.

---

very popular among nationalist African leaders because it offered a way for them to overcome both regionalism and ethnic divides by stressing commonalities and a common oppression.

The Year of Africa, the year of the release of the greatest number of colonies, was declared in 1960. For most of the countries of Africa, independence was the end result of mass demonstrations and strikes, negotiations, and in some cases, decisions of the United Nations. However, the proclamation of the independence of Kenya, Zimbabwe, Angola, Mozambique, and Namibia was preceded by war, insurrection, and guerrilla warfare.

The years following independence were not always easy. Natural resources had been plundered, little infrastructure was built, most countries had little preparation for self-rule, and there was conflict among ethnic groups. In many countries, dictators came to power, with a blatant disregard for human rights. In turn, there was much economic upheaval and growing poverty.

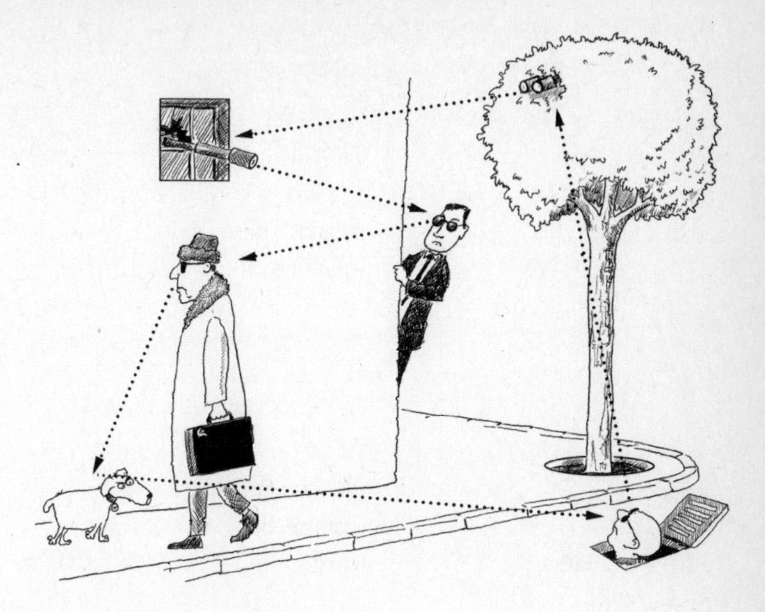

The Cold War

At the wartime summit meetings of Yalta and Potsdam, serious tensions emerged between the United States, Britain, and the Soviet Union over the future of Germany and Eastern Europe. America especially feared the spread of Soviet power and Communism. This fear intensified when the Soviet Union went on to set up satellite republics in Poland (despite having promised to honor free and fair elections), Czechoslovakia, and Hungary, thus extending the Eastern bloc of Soviet-controlled states. The Soviet blockade of Berlin in 1948–1949 (during which supplies had to be airlifted into the city by British and American planes), and the eventual division of Germany between east and west further soured relationships.

ECHOES OF THE PAST

History is a relentless master. It has no present, only the past rushing into the future. To try to hold fast is to be swept aside.

—John F. Kennedy (1917–1963)

Over the next few decades, as the United States and the Soviet Union rushed to develop nuclear weapons, tension between the superpowers remained high. The Berlin Wall was constructed in 1961 to prevent mass defection of Communist East Germans to the West. The darkest moment in the Cold War was the **Cuban Missile Crisis** in 1962. The world held its breath for a week as the United States under President **John F. Kennedy** successfully faced off the Soviet Union's ambition to base nuclear missiles in Cuba. Tension also intensified in the 1980s when President **Ronald Reagan** initiated the development of the **Strategic Defense Initiative** (or Star Wars), a system designed to destroy any missiles aimed at the United States.

Because neither power actually wanted a nuclear Armageddon, the United States and Russia used **proxy conflicts** to advance their global influence, with Russia sending troops to support Communist rule in Afghanistan, Hungary, Czechoslovakia, and East Germany. Meanwhile, the United States helped to overthrow the Communist government in Guatemala, backed an invasion of Cuba, supported the Contras (*contrarevolucionarios*) against the socialist Sandinistas in a civil war in Nicaragua, and invaded the Dominican Republic and Grenada. The United States was particularly concerned about the "domino effect" of states falling to Communism in Southeast Asia and became involved in two costly and largely unsuccessful wars.

NATO

The North Atlantic Treaty Organization (NATO) was formed in 1949 as a military alliance between Western European countries, the United States, and Canada, originally against the perceived threat of Soviet aggression. With their headquarters in Brussels, 12 member states agreed that "an armed attack against one or more of them in Europe or North America shall be considered an attack upon them all." Another 16 nations have since joined, including countries from the former Eastern bloc. To counter NATO, in 1955 the Soviet Union formed its own alliance—the Warsaw Pact—with countries of Eastern Europe.

The Korean War (1950–1953)

At the end of World War II, Korea, which had been occupied by the Japanese, was divided into the Soviet-occupied North and the United States–occupied South. The respective occupying forces withdrew in 1949. In 1950, North Korea invaded South Korea. Fearing the spread of Communism in Southeast Asia, the United States and sixteen other U.N. member states sent forces under the command of General Douglas MacArthur to aid the South, while Chinese troops fought on behalf of the North. By June 1951 there was a stalemate; in 1953 an armistice was signed, reinstating the original boundaries.

The Vietnam War (1965–1975)

Vietnam was also divided into two states by the Treaty of Geneva in 1954: North Vietnam under the Communist government of Ho Chi Minh and South Vietnam under a government that was friendly to the West. In 1961 the United States began to send increased military aid to South Vietnam to help it remove the Vietcong, a Communist guerrilla movement backed by the North that had been fighting to overthrow the government of South Vietnam. The United States made direct intervention in 1964 following claims that North Vietnamese forces had attacked a U.S. spy ship in the area.

By 1967 there were 500,000 U.S. troops in Vietnam fighting the Vietcong. In January 1968, the Communists launched the Tet Offensive, which was eventually driven back. But as U.S. casualties grew, it became clear that the United States could not win the war. Mounting costs and opposition to the war at home eventually led President **Richard M. Nixon** to pull out of Vietnam. In 1973 a ceasefire was agreed (though fighting continued). In 1975 North Vietnam and the Vietcong conquered South Vietnam and united it under Communism: a humiliating defeat for the United States, a so-called superpower. Millions of Vietnamese died in the war.

The End of the Communist Era in Europe

As the Cold War rumbled on, opposition to the Communist regime in the Eastern bloc gained momentum, first in Poland and then in Hungary in 1956, where an uprising was brutally repressed and a hard-line Communist government established. In 1968 a new leader, **Alexander Dubček,** tried to reform the Stalinist state of Czechoslovakia, although he was eventually removed and the country remained under Soviet control.

The advent of **Mikhail Gorbachev** as Soviet leader in 1985 signaled the beginning of liberalization. Gorbachev launched a series of policies designed to revive an ailing state through *perestroika* (a restructuring of the economy) and *glasnost* (openness to new ideas and freedom of speech). Relations between Moscow and Washington improved as Gorbachev directed Soviet resources away from the arms race and toward reviving the economy. In 1987 the Intermediate-Range Nuclear Forces Treaty limited U.S. and Soviet nuclear arsenals.

As part of his new economic policy, Gorbachev made it clear in 1988 that Soviet forces would no longer crush dissent in Communist regimes. Both Hungary and Poland took advantage of this, with multi-party elections, followed by the establishment of the non-Communist Solidarity movement in Poland, led by **Lech Walesa.** Czechoslovakia, Bulgaria, and Romania removed their Communist governments. In East Germany, a tidal wave of street protests led to the fall of the Berlin Wall in 1989 and the eventual reunification of Germany in 1990.

The collapse of Communism in the Eastern bloc accelerated as fifteen Soviet republics declared independence from the Union by 1991. In August 1991 a group of hard-line Communists staged a coup against Gorbachev. **Boris Yeltsin,** then the leader of a key industrial area of Russia, put the coup down, and the Communist Party was banned. Gorbachev resigned on Christmas Day 1991, the Soviet Union was dissolved, and Yeltsin became leader of an independent Russia, his official title being President of the Russian Federation. Communism had collapsed, leading many to declare that the Cold War was also at an end.

The Last Great Communist State

After World War II, civil war in China between the Nationalists (backed by the United States) and the Communists (backed by popular support) resumed. Mao Zedong declared victory for the **People's Republic of China** in 1949, and the Nationalists retreated to Taiwan (then called Formosa). Chinese troops continued to claim additional territory, expanding into Mongolia and Tibet.

Mao attempted to transform China into a modern socialist state by seizing land from private ownership and creating collective farms. He also nationalized all private industry. The first Five Year Plan resulted in increased industrial output.

> **ECHOES OF THE PAST**
>
> I have witnessed the tremendous energy of the masses. On this foundation it is possible to accomplish any task whatsoever.
>
> —Mao Zedong (1893–1976)

He followed that initial success with the Great Leap Forward, from 1958 to 1962. A lack of technology and a series of bad harvests undermined industrial output and agricultural output, and the country suffered economically. Millions starved to death. This period was followed by the Cultural Revolution, 1966–1976, a time of great repression.

After the death of Mao in 1979, a program of economic liberalism was instituted, developing China into the second-largest economy in the world, after the United States. It has been the world's fastest-growing major economy, with consistent growth rates of around 10 percent over the past 30 years. China is also the largest exporter and second-largest importer of goods in the world, with a consumer market of 1.3 billion people. Because China is such an important player on the global financial stage, it is able to advance its foreign policy goals through economic activity. Some experts predict that China is poised to be the next global superpower.

The War on Terror

On September 11, 2001, planes slammed into the World Trade Center towers in New York City and damaged the Pentagon in Washington, D.C. A group called **Al-Qaeda,** under the direction of **Osama bin Laden**, claimed responsibility. Al-Qaeda is a worldwide militant Islamist terrorist organization founded by Osama bin Laden sometime in the late 1980s. It operates as a network of multinationals and it calls for global jihad. (Jihad is defined as a holy war on behalf of Islam.) It has been designated a "terrorist organization" by the United States, the United Nations Security Council, the European Union, NATO, and various other countries.

Before the attacks of 9/11, Al-Qaeda attacked civilian and military targets in several countries. The group claimed responsibility for a hotel bombing in Yemen in 1992, which targeted U.S. troops en route to Somalia; a 1993 World Trade Center bombing that took place in an underground parking garage; the 1998 U.S. embassy bombings in Kenya and Dar es Salaam; and the 2000 bombing of the USS *Cole,* among others.

Under President George W. Bush, the United States declared a "war on terror" and invaded both Iraq and Afghanistan. The way the war on terror has been conducted has led to concerns about its impact on civil liberties and the cost of the war. Osama bin Laden was eventually tracked down and killed 10 years after the 9/11 attacks.

Global Interdependence

Today the world is interconnected through mass communications, computer technology, and rapid transportation. Human population has reached 7 billion, and more than 50 percent of those humans live in cities, a trend that seems certain to continue. The Industrial Revolution that began in the 1800s continues with the accelerating use of coal, petroleum, and natural gas. The environmental effects of human actions have accumulated drastically, with massive deforestation, land degradation, atmospheric pollution, the extinction of species, the fouling of the world's oceans and rivers, and global warming.

Global trade impacts the entire world, but there is a huge discrepancy between the wealth and standards of living enjoyed by nations in North America and Europe compared with those of other nations. Television and the Internet have ended cultural isolation for many people, and traditional cultures have felt under attack. Economic disruptions and war have led to huge increases in immigration.

ECHOES OF THE PAST

Our loyalties must transcend our race, our tribe, our class, and our nations, and this means we must develop a world perspective.

—Martin Luther King, Jr. (1929–1968)

For better or worse, humans have been forced into closer interdependence than ever before. For some, this has brought new prosperity; for others there has been the destruction of cherished traditions.

Chapter 11

A Brief Time Line

c. 5000–2000 B.C. Sumer civilization in southern Mesopotamia

c. 3200 B.C. Ancient Egypt emerges in Nile valley

c. 3000 B.C. Minoan civilization forms in Crete

c. 2550–2470 B.C. Pyramids of Giza built in Egypt

c. 2500 B.C. Civilization arises along the Indus River

c. 2000–539 B.C. Babylonian empire thrives

c. 2000 B.C. Hittite empire emerges in the Mediterranean

c. 1600 B.C.	Shang dynasty emerges in China
c. 1500 B.C.	Olmec civilization emerges in South America
c. 1200 B.C.	Writing emerges in China
c. 1190 B.C.	Hittite empire disintegrates
c. 1046 B.C.	Zhou dynasty comes to power in China
c. 900 B.C.	Celts appear in Gaul, Spain, and British Isles
c. 750 B.C.	Greek city-states emerge
600 B.C.	City of Rome is established
550 B.C.	Cyrus the Great establishes the kingdom of Persia
539 B.C.	Babylon becomes part of the Persian Empire
509 B.C.	Rome becomes a republic

508 B.C.	Athens established as a democracy
499–449 B.C.	Persian Wars
486 B.C.	Persian Empire reaches greatest extent
447–432 B.C.	The Parthenon is built in Athens
338 B.C.	Philip II of Macedonia conquers Greece
332 B.C.	Alexander the Great conquers Egypt
300 B.C.	Mayan civilization emerges in Central America
264–146 B.C.	Punic Wars between Rome and Carthage

221 B.C. Qin dynasty begins first united empire in China

146 B.C. Greek peninsula comes under Roman rule

31 B.C. Battle of Actium

30 B.C. Rome conquers Egypt

27 B.C. Augustus becomes first Roman emperor

A.D. 67 Buddhism arrives in China

A.D. 97–117 Roman Empire reaches its greatest extent

A.D. 320 Gupta empire emerges in India

A.D. 324 Byzantine Empire established

A.D. 610 Islam emerges with the teachings of the Prophet Muhammad

A.D. 618 Tang dynasty begins in China

A.D. 750 Golden age of Islam and the Abbasid Caliphate

A.D. 800 Charlemagne crowned Holy Roman emperor

A.D. 960 Song dynasty begins in China

1054 Eastern Orthodox Church formed

1066 Battle of Hastings

1071 Turks capture Byzantium

1095–1291 The Crusades fought in the Holy Land

1190–1192 Richard I on Crusade

1192 First Japanese shogunate

1215 Magna Carta signed by King John

c. 1250 Aztec conquest in Central America

1271 Kublai Khan establishes the Yuan dynasty in China

1326 Ottoman Empire established

1337–1453 The Hundred Years' War

1348 Black Death arrives in Europe

1368 Ming dynasty begins in China and expels all foreigners

1381 Peasants' Revolt

1400s Incas conquer much of South America

1415 English victory at Agincourt

1429 English defeated by Joan of Arc at Orléans

1453 Constantinople falls to the Ottoman Turks

1478 Spanish Inquisition set up by Pope Sixtus IV

1492 Christopher Columbus discovers the New World

1494 Mughal Empire established in India

1497 John Cabot lands on Newfoundland in the New World

1498 Vasco da Gama discovers sea route to East Indies

1499 Safavid empire established in Persia

1499–1502 Amerigo Vespucci makes voyages to the Americas

1509 Henry VIII becomes king of England

1517 Martin Luther's ninety-five theses spark the Reformation

1520 Magellan circumnavigates the globe

1520 Cortés conquers Mexico

1532 Pizarro conquers the Incas

1534 Henry VIII breaks with Rome and establishes the Church of England

1547 Reign of Ivan the Terrible in Russia begins

1553 Mary I becomes queen of England

1558 Elizabeth I becomes queen of England

1559 The Acts of Supremacy and Uniformity

1577–1580 Francis Drake circumnavigates the world

1584 First (unsuccessful) Virginia colony established

1588 English defeat of the Spanish Armada

1600 English East India Company given a royal charter

1602 Dutch East India Company founded

1603 James I becomes first joint monarch of Scotland and England

1607 First permanent English colony established at Jamestown, Virginia

1611 King James Bible published

1618 Start of Thirty Years' War

1620 Pilgrims set sail on the *Mayflower*

1625 Charles I becomes king of England

1642–1649 British Civil War

1648	End of Thirty Years' War
1649–1660	Cromwell's Commonwealth
1660	Charles II restored to the throne
1670	Hudson's Bay Company founded in Canada
1689	English Bill of Rights
1696	Peter the Great ascends the throne in Russia
1701–1713	War of the Spanish Succession
1707	Acts of Union
1769–1770	Captain Cook sails to New Zealand and Australia

1776	Declaration of Independence in America
1788	First penal colony established in Australia
1789–1799	French Revolution
1792–1815	French Revolutionary and Napoleonic Wars
1801	Second Act of Union results in the formation of the United Kingdom

1803	United States purchases Louisiana Territory from the French
1804	Napoleon becomes emperor of France
1804	Haiti becomes an independent republic
1812–1815	War of 1812

1815	Napoleon defeated at Battle of Waterloo
1821	Mexico declares independence from Spain
1833	Slavery abolished in British colonies
1837	Queen Victoria ascends the throne of England
1839–1842	First Opium War
1845–1852	Irish potato famine
1848	First gold rush in California
1853–1856	Crimean War
1855	Livingstone discovers Victoria Falls in Africa
1856–1860	Second Opium War
1857–1858	Indian Mutiny
1861–1865	American Civil War

1865	Slavery abolished in United States
1868	Meiji Restoration in Japan
1869	Transcontinental railroad completed in United States
1870–1871	Franco-Prussian War
1880–1881	First Boer War
1882	Germany forms Triple Alliance with Austria-Hungary and Italy
1889	Brazil becomes an independent republic
1893	Women given the vote in New Zealand
1894–1895	First Sino-Japanese War
1899–1902	Second Boer War
1900	Boxer Rebellion in China
1901	Australia becomes a state of the British Commonwealth
1904	Anglo-French Entente Cordiale
1904–1905	Russo-Japanese War
1905	Russian Revolution of 1905
1907	New Zealand becomes a self-governing dominion
1912	Kuomintang overthrows the Qing dynasty in China

1914 Irish Home Rule Act

1914 World War I begins

1916 Easter Rising in Dublin

1917 Russian revolutions

1918 World War I ends

1918 Women granted the vote in United Kingdom

1918 Bolsheviks sue for peace with Germany

1918 Surrender of Ottoman Empire

1919 Treaty of Versailles

1919 League of Nations established

1919 Mussolini founds Italian Fascist movement

1919–1921 Irish War of Independence

1920 Women granted the vote in the United States

1920 Communist Party established in China

1921 Irish Free State established

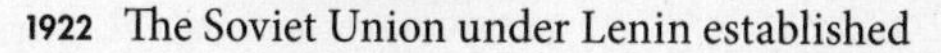

1922 The Soviet Union under Lenin established

1922–1923 Civil war in Ireland

1925 Persia becomes Iran and begins modernizing

1927 Stalin becomes Soviet leader

1928 Chiang Kai-shek becomes president of the Nationalist Republic of China

1929	Wall Street stock market crashes, setting off a worldwide depression
1933	Hitler comes to power in Germany
1935	Italy invades Abyssinia
1936–1938	Stalin's Great Purges
1936	Spanish Civil War begins
1937	Second Sino-Japanese War begins

1939	World War II begins
1939	Spanish Civil War ends
1940	France surrenders to Germany
1941	America and Russia enter the war
1944	D-Day landings in Normandy
1945	Victory in Europe
1945	Atomic bombs dropped on Hiroshima and Nagasaki
1945	World War II ends
1945	The United Nations established
1945	Potsdam Conference and partition of Germany
1947	State of Israel created
1947	Partition of India
1948	Republic of Ireland (Eire) declared
1948–1949	Soviet blockade of Berlin

1949 NATO formed

1949 People's Republic of China established by Chairman Mao

1950–1953 Korean War

1955 Warsaw Pact signed

1956 Hungarian Uprising

1960 Year of Africa; thirteen former colonies gain independence

1961 Berlin Wall built

1965–1975 Vietnam War

1985 Mikhail Gorbachev becomes Soviet leader

1989 Collapse of Berlin Wall

1990 Reunification of Germany

1991 Soviet Union is dissolved; Boris Yeltsin becomes leader of independent Russia

1996 End of apartheid in South Africa

2001 Attacks on World Trade Center

Index

ENJOY THESE OTHER READER'S DIGEST BESTSELLERS

I Used to Know That

Make learning fun again with these lighthearted pages that are packed with important theories, phrases, and those long-forgotten "rules" you once learned in school.

Caroline Taggart
ISBN 978-0-7621-0995-1

I Used to Know That: Geography

It's hard to know everything about the interaction of diverse physical, biological, and cultural features of the Earth's surface. Explore all of it with this entertaining, easy-to-understand little book.

Will Williams

ISBN 978-1-60652-245-5

I Used to Know That: Civil War

Taking you beyond the history book, these pages bring to life colorful personal stories of heroes, brilliant military strategists, blunderers, guerillas, outright villains, spies, secret sympathizers on both sides, and their wives on the home front.

Fred DuBose
ISBN 978-1-60652-244-8

I Used to Know That: Shakespeare

Capturing the unbelievable scope of Shakespeare's influence, this book will surprise and delight you not only with fascinating facts and little-known details of his life but also with the surprising legacy of the language and phrases inherited from his works.

Liz Evers
ISBN 978-1-60652-246-2

I Used to Know That: Philosophy

Spanning over 2,000 years of philosophical thought, this book covers the main highlights, from Pythagoras to Socrates to Sartre. You'll get an overview of all the major theories, presented in an engaging format.

Lesley Levene

ISBN 978-1-60652-323-0

E=MC²

Anyone frightened by the subject of physics will learn that quantum mechanics doesn't bite—even if it does occasionally bang. Packed with amusing examples, this lively book distills all of the most important discoveries of physics.

Jeff Stewart

ISBN 978-1-60652-167-0

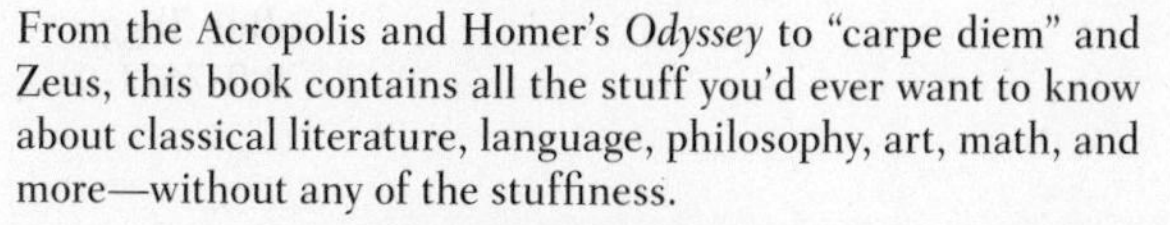

The Classics

From the Acropolis and Homer's *Odyssey* to "carpe diem" and Zeus, this book contains all the stuff you'd ever want to know about classical literature, language, philosophy, art, math, and more—without any of the stuffiness.

Caroline Taggart

ISBN 978-1-60652-132-8

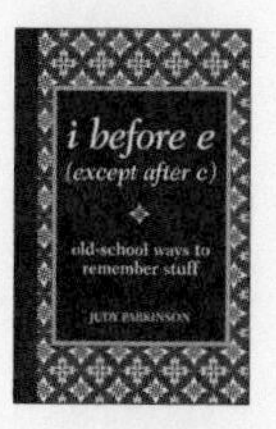

i before e (except after c)

Featuring all the memory-jogging tips you'll ever need to know, this fun little book will help you recall hundreds of important facts using simple, easy-to-remember mnemonics from your schooldays.

Judy Parkinson

ISBN 978-0-7621-0917-3

DON'T FORGET THESE BESTSELLERS

A Certain "Je Ne Sais Quoi"

Easy as Pi

Spilling the Beans on the Cat's Pajamas

Each Book is $14.95 hardcover

For more information visit us at RDTradePublishing.com

E-book editions also available.

Reader's Digest books can be purchased through retail and online bookstores. In the United States books are distributed by Penguin Group (USA), Inc. For more information or to order books, call 1-800-788-6262.

Bengala
Borneo
I. Pulotigas
P. Condor
Cambodia
Tsiompa
Celebes
Manado
Mindoro
Carchi
Iunnan
INDOSTAN
Cabul
Samarchand
A S I A
Sigan
Philippinæ Insulæ
C. del Spirito Santo
C. del Engano
I. Formosa
I.S. Ioannes
I. dos Matelotes
OCEANVS
CHINENSIS
I. dos Arecifes
I. de Bidimas
I. Aves
Ilhas de Ladrones
Malabrigo
Miracomo Vuz
I. Fungma
I. Fuego
Malabrigo
I. das Hermanos
Quiocouni
I. Iapon
Uno Coluna
I. Grifima
C. Eroen
TARTARIA
TANGVT
CATHAYA
Cambalu
Strat de Vries
C. Bitiantie
Compagnis Landt
Las dos Hermanos
Los Iardines
Nadadores
I. Corales
de las Vesinos
de Pasaros
I. dos Reiz
Barbudos
Baixos de S. Bartholomæ
I. de S. Pedro
Circulus sub Tropico Cancri
Circulus sub Æquatore
Linea sub Circulo Arctico
ANIAN
Stret Anian
C. Mendocino
Nova Albion
P. de Sr. Fr. Draco
C. de Galera
I. d. S. Augustin
California
Pt. del Engano
P. de la Trinidad
Los Monges
La Desgraciada
I. a Rocca partida
C. de S. Lucas
C. de Corrientes
Nova Granada
Pueblos de Moqui
140
150
210
220